English Country Churches

Also by Richard Briers and published by Robson Books
Coward and Company

ENGLISH COUNTRY CHURCHES

Richard Briers

Photographs by Mervyn Blatch

 Robson Books

Acknowledgements

The author and publishers would like to express their thanks to the Historic Churches Preservation Trust for their help in the preparation of this book and to Mervyn Blatch who supplied the photographs.

First published in Great Britain in 1989 by Robson Books Ltd, Bolsover House, 5–6 Clipstone Street, London W1P 7EB

British Library Cataloguing in Publication Data
Briers, Richard, 1934 –
  A guide to English country churches.
  1. England. Rural regions. Churches
  I. Title
  942

ISBN 0 86051 606 7

Typeset by Selectmove Ltd. London

Printed in Great Britain by
Butler & Tanner Ltd, Frome and London

Contents

Foreword

My mother's side of the family is deeply rooted in the church, though when I was a child I always found church buildings rather spooky. As a fourteen-year-old I decided that I had better hang up my surplice in Christ Church, Wimbledon after it became apparent that my calling as a server was to the greater glory of Briers and not the greater glory of the Almighty. Then I went to drama school and played Everyman in the crypt of St Paul's (where I gather I am entitled to marry off my daughters, should I or they so wish, thanks to my OBE). After Everyman came the occasional role of a parson later in my career. So one way and another I have had a nodding acquaintance with the church both inside and out for most of my life.

It's only recently that this has developed into an awareness of what churches – and country churches in particular – have to offer even the casual visitor. At a time when those all-important moments of tranquillity and reflection become increasingly hard to find, sitting quietly in the cool of a building that has been standing for a quarter of the Christian era, or longer, helps one put life into perspective.

In a church you find a sense of continuity. The same surnames appear on headstones and memorials. In many churches you can see a gradual process of development and change in the building itself – a process that is refreshingly active today as churches around the country open their doors to flower festivals and concerts. They open them as well to growing numbers of visitors interested in discovering something of our past through one of the most readily accessible sources. Visiting a country church is like opening a window on living history; inside every one and around every churchyard the past is always present.

With 10,000 medieval churches alone in England, selecting just one hundred is an awesome and frankly impossible task. To achieve some balance, almost every English county is represented here (and listed with its respective churches at the back). Many of those included are outstanding buildings which reveal so much about our ecclesiastical and social history that they fall into any enthusiast's list of leading English Churches. Several like Cirencester, Grantham and Hexham are town churches that act as a focal point for the rural areas in which they lie – stretching the definition of 'country' just a little, but allowing the inclusion of some of our finest parish churches.

Others are superb examples of a particular style of church architecture, or contain wonderful works of ecclesiastical art or decoration. There are churches like Deerhurst, Greensted and Lindisfarne deeply rooted in our history. Then there are those with special connections with famous figures of the past – Wordsworth with Grasmere, Gilbert White with Selborne, Dr Johnson and David Garrick with Easton Maudit.

Finally comes an intriguing group of churches, often obscure or off the beaten track, that have an idiosyncratic appeal all of their own, whether they commemorate the shortest saint ever canonized, or retain their patron saint's relics, or simply provide the final resting-place for the last Fool in England.

However, the maintenance of these and the thousands of other churches – the majority of which are well worth a visit – is a formidable challenge and one in which the Historic Churches Preservation Trust at Fulham Palace is playing a vital leading role. For future generations to benefit as we have from our rich ecclesiastical heritage, the Trust merits the support of everyone who has discovered the fascinating clues to both past and present that lie below every beckoning spire and inside every studded oak door.

All the photographs in this book are the work of Mervyn Blatch, who is a leading authority on English country churches and also a member of the General Committee of the Incorporated Church Building Society.

Richard Briers

ARCHITECTURAL PERIODS AND CHARACTERISTICS

Saxon: before the Norman Conquest (1066). The earliest churches were frequently made of timber.

Norman: Romanesque architecture of the 11th and 12th centuries, characterized by round arches, heavy pillars, massive masonry walls etc.

Early English: 13th century – first stage of English Gothic, with pointed arches, lancet windows and simple tracery.

Decorated: 14th century – second stage of English Gothic, with geometrical tracery and floral decoration.

Perpendicular: 15th century – third stage of English Gothic, with vertical tracery in large windows.

One architectural style and period runs into another, of course – as many of the churches in this book show.

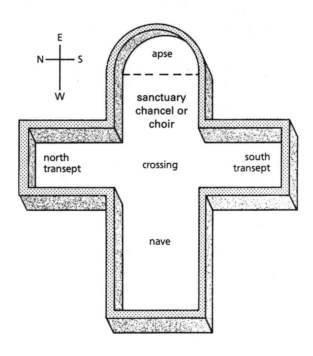

Holy Trinity and St Mary, Abbey Dore, Hereford and Worcester

2 MILES NORTH OF PONTRILAS ON B4347

Abbey Dore lies beside the River Dore in the tranquil surroundings of the Golden Valley in the west of the former county of Herefordshire. This is a gentle landscape of orchards and wooded hills against which the massive red sandstone church stands as a vivid reminder of the wealth of monastic orders in England before their dissolution under Henry VIII.

Cistercians founded the abbey in 1147 and thirty-three years later work began on the present building, removing all traces of the church that had formerly stood on the site. The new structure contained a *presbytery* (eastern part of the church kept for the use of the clergy), crossing, north and south transepts with four chapels each on their eastern ends, and a nave 152 feet long with north and south aisles. A short time later the presbytery was extended and aisles were added on the north and south sides together with a further aisle behind the high altar known as an *ambulatory*. The east walls of the two inner chapels were removed to provide access to the new aisles and the former east end of the presbytery was replaced by the beautifully designed arcade of three bays.

After the suppression of the abbey in 1535 the church soon fell into disrepair. This and the abbey lands passed to the Scudamore family and almost a century later the

1

first Viscount Scudamore set about repairing the building, now standing in ruins and acting as a makeshift
cowshed. The work he undertook was through necessity
fairly drastic. The arches leading into the nave and side
aisles had to be blocked, reducing the length of the church
by more than half. John Abel, a celebrated Herefordshire
carpenter, was engaged to build a new roof in local oak
and a mason from Ross-on-Wye undertook to build the
present tower and two buttresses for just over £100.

Viscount Scudamore's restoration took two years to
complete and on Palm Sunday 1634, just short of a
century after the abbey had been abandoned, the church
was reconsecrated as the parish church, making it one of
the very few Cistercian abbeys, if not the only one, to be
used as a parish church today.

Since then what was left of the other monastic buildings and cloisters on the north side of the church, and
most of the nave, has all but disappeared from sight.

Although when seen from the outside the changes
made to the church's original design present a rather
confused picture, accentuated by the 17th-century tower,
once inside the simplicity and grandeur speak for themselves. The transepts and crossing are lofty, spacious
and uncluttered. The walls are painted with late 17th-
and early 18th-century texts and designs, including the
arms of Queen Anne. There is a sturdy minstrels' gallery
against the blocked centre west arch that formerly led
into the nave, and in the western corner of the north
wall is a blocked doorway through which the monks
would have entered the church by steps down from their
dormitory for their night-time services.

John Abel also carved the handsome oak screen through
which you enter the presbytery, adding the three coats of
arms of Charles I in the centre, with those of the
Scudamores to the north and Archbishop Laud to the
south. Ahead, at the eastern end, is the lovely Early

English arcade, simple and unadorned, which is one of the most outstanding features of this noble building. The altar, a massive feature measuring twelve feet in length, was salvaged and restored to the church by Viscount Scudamore after it had been found in a farm building where it had served as a salting-bench and cheese-table for the best part of a hundred years! The floor on either side of the altar is decorated with 13th-century tiles bearing the arms of benefactors of the church which were discovered in various places and laid here during restoration work at the beginning of this century.

The ambulatory, which now contains some fine carved bosses and other pieces of decorated masonry rescued from the ruined nave, shows the remains of five chapels which once stood against the east wall.

In the south aisle there is a large stone coffin, and under one of the arches a 12th-century figure of Robert Fitzharold, the founder of the church, dressed in armour. Until a few years ago this figure was life-size and then someone pinched the upper portion, leaving poor Sir Robert headless.

There's an Early English doorway on the north side of the church, which is worth looking at for its elaborate hinges; one of them shows the head of an animal thought to be a wolf. According to some authorities, this may recall an order issued by Edward I that all wolves in Herefordshire and the counties bordering it were to be hunted down and killed, reminding us that the peaceful rural backwater we enjoy today was once the home of wild animals that we associate with northern Canada or the wilds of Siberia.

St Mary the Virgin, Abbotts Ann, Hampshire

Abbotts Ann is a pretty Hampshire village that has a long history dating back to before the Roman conquest. The church holds a parish register with entries starting in 1561, though the present building is some century and a half younger. It is for its collection of funerary garlands that St Mary's is particularly noteworthy and the oldest of these is only some thirty years younger than the church itself.

Four of the five bells from the old church were incorporated into the new building but otherwise the Georgian church, built at his own expense by Thomas Pitt, forebear of the famous Prime Minister, completely replaced its predecessor. The squire's family pew, the gallery, font and pulpit are fine examples from their period. The stained-glass windows are a 19th-century addition.

The funerary garlands (or virgins' crowns, as they are also called) hang near the ceiling on either side of the church, the vestiges of a custom dating from the Middle Ages. These were presented at the funeral of unmarried men or women who were born, baptized and died in the parish and who, in the words of Gilbert White, the celebrated naturalist and parson from Selborne, were 'reputed to have died virgins'.

The garlands are made of hazel, decorated with paper

4

rosettes. Paper gauntlets hang below, offering a challenge to anyone who cared to question the deceased's 'qualifications' for the honour.

At the funeral two young girls dressed in white would carry the garland suspended on a pole. After the service it would be hung from the gallery in the church, so that everyone entering would pass beneath it. If after three weeks no challenge had been made, the garland was hung on a bracket near the ceiling with a note of the deceased person's name and dates. There it would remain until age and decay brought about its downfall, and the oldest, as I've said, are still there after 250 years.

Recipients of the garlands have been commemorated more recently by the beautifully embroidered kneelers that ladies of the parish have made for this delightful church.

St Nonna, Altarnun, Cornwall

The parish of Altarnun, or Altarnon to give its original, correct spelling, is the largest in Cornwall and its fine Perpendicular church stands confidently at its heart as it has done since the Middle Ages.

The church's commanding presence and its position on the north-eastern flank of Bodmin Moor have earned St Nonna's the name 'The Cathedral of the Moor'. However, the present church is only the most recent on a site of ancient worship that stretches back to the time of St Nonna, the Celtic saint to whom the church is dedicated and after whom the village was named as the 'altar of St Non (or Nonna)'.

Nonna was the Christian daughter of a chieftain ruling in south-west Wales early in the 6th century. The son to whom she gave birth was named Dewi, or David, and was destined to become the patron saint of Wales; there is a holy well dedicated to St Non not far from St David's Cathedral. St Nonna is also the patron of a parish near Looe and one in Brittany, as well as that of Altarnon – evidence that places St David's mother among the band of Celtic missionaries who travelled from Wales and Ireland to continental Europe, by way of Cornwall, in the 6th and 7th centuries.

The evangelism of these early saints is graphically recalled in the churchyard of St Nonna's; by the church gate stands a fine Celtic cross, believed to date from the

6

6th century and marking the site as holy ground for the best part of 1,500 years.

St Nonna's original church has long since disappeared and so has most of the Norman building erected in the early 12th century. The only substantial remnant from this is the font, which typifies the late Romanesque style. It is square, unlike earlier Norman fonts which favoured the rounded Saxon shape. There are striking carved faces at the corners and rosettes on the sides.

Building work began on the present church early in the 15th century, using in part moorstone, lumps of granite found lying on the open moors. Though immensely durable, granite does not yield easily to the mason's chisel and for this reason the pillars in St Nonna's were shaped from single blocks of stone, as were the capitals and bases.

As befits this spacious church the wagon roofs (designed in the shape of a medieval wagon canopy) are lofty and grand. But the most interesting wooden features are unquestionably the bench ends, seventy-nine in all, that were carved over a period of twenty years early in the 16th century. These were the work of Robart Daye, whose signature appears on the bench end nearest the font. He chose a wide range of subjects, from orthodox Christian symbols like the cross and the ladders to heraldic designs, and from scenes of local life such as shepherding to musicians – he even depicted a man playing the bagpipes!

In the 16th century the church also possessed an imposing *rood screen* (a carved wooden or stone screen that separated the chancel from the nave and supported the crucifix, or *rood*) which was replaced by the existing one a century ago, making use of some of the timber from its predecessor. The original rood screen must have been quite a structure. It was possible to walk along it; indeed, it was customary for the Gospel to be sung from it during mass.

The chancel has a 17th-century altar rail, stretching the width of the church, which bears a lengthy inscription.

The tower of St Nonna's stands over 100 feet high and is reckoned to be the third highest in Cornwall. Inside you can still see the deep holes where the masons lodged their scaffolding beams during its construction.

As a final reminder of St Nonna, not too far away there's a well named after her which was believed to cure insanity. Lunatics were plunged into it and then taken to the church, where masses were said over them in the hope that they would regain their wits. In the cases of those who did, prayers of thanks were offered to the saint. The others presumably returned to the well at a later stage for another immersion.

St John the Baptist, Ashton, Devon

There are many things to commend Ashton church. It
stands in a lovely setting on the western slopes of Haldon
hill overlooking the Teign valley. The restoration work
that took place at the end of the last century displays
a sensitivity often absent from the Victorian work in
many other churches. And, above all else, Ashton has
some of the very best medieval screen-painting in the
West of England.

The church dates from the 15th century and its design and furnishings reflect work that spans most of
that century. There is a studded oak door in the south
porch made of two layers of planks braced in alternate
directions. The ceilings of the south porch and nave
were originally built in the wagon-roof style. There are
carved bench ends from the same period. And the font
and arcade that separates the north aisle from the nave
are worked from Beer stone, quarried at Beer on the coast
near Seaton, in a style typical of the 15th century too.

Ashton's principal attractions, though, are its carved
and painted screens. A *parclose screen* divides the chancel from the chapel in the north aisle and the *rood screen*
is still in place, spanning the whole of the nave and aisle.
The *rood loft* which would have sat on top of the screen
was still there early in the last century, but it has since
been taken down; stairs behind the pulpit would have

given access to it. The rood seen in the church today was carved in 1915.

The lower tier of the screen consists of thirty-two panels, with painted figures grouped in fours. The saints depicted are each shown with their appropriate emblems, though some are more immediately recognizable than others. Saints George and Michael are both shown slaying dragons. St Mark, St Matthew and St Luke are shown carrying books and accompanied by their respective symbols of lion, angel and ox. Among other familiar saints, St Lawrence is there with his gridiron and St Sebastian bristling uncomfortably with arrows. However, others like St Blaise, St Leodegar and St Sybil might not have been so immediately identified down the years.

At least one of the saints shown has a particular local connection. This is St Sidwell (the sixteenth figure running from north to south), who is shown carrying a scythe. Tradition holds that this early believer was martyred by haymakers outside Exeter in the 7th century, and a spring apparently bubbled from the ground at the place where her blood was shed. The site is remembered today in Sidwell Street in the eastern part of Exeter. Much the same story is told of St Urith of Chittlehampton and, since two figures appear carrying scythes at Ashton, it is possible that one of them represents this saint from the northern part of the county.

In addition to the paintings in the aisle portion of the rood screen those that form the eastern face in the north aisle chapel and the ones on the parclose screen are even more striking. They date from slightly later than the nave paintings and show figures dressed in costumes of the 16th century. Each painting bears a Latin inscription connected with the story of the Incarnation.

The north aisle chapel at one time housed the vault of the Chudliegh family, lords of the manor from the early 14th century until the middle of the 18th century and whose arms decorate the font, some of the original medieval glass and a number of monuments around the church. Until the turn of this century the wooden monument now on the north wall of the aisle hung over the vault. When this was removed the remains of a 15th-century wall painting came to light, which showed the figure of Christ standing in front of the cross, showing his wounds and surrounded by the instruments of the Passion. (St Mary, Astbury, has angels with shields displaying these – see page 16.) The picture was still clearly discernible in the early years of this century.

St Mary, Ashwell, Hertfordshire

There are ash trees and a 'well', or spring, from which gurgle the headwaters of the River Rhee, the principal tributary of the Cam, in the ancient village of Ashwell which in Norman times was the sixth largest town in Hertfordshire.

Ashwell is rich in buildings of all periods stretching back to the Middle Ages, with the tower of St Mary's Church as its crowning glory, rising to a height of 176 feet and topped by the distinctive small leaded spire found throughout the county and known as a 'Herts spike'.

St Mary's was built during the 14th century, towards the end of the Decorated period of church architecture. It has a bright, airy interior, due to the absence of stained glass, and this comprises a large aisleless chancel and a nave where faint traces of murals have been detected under the whitewash. Overall the interior reflects a steady progress from east to west over the period of half a century.

Where St Mary's may lack the number of formal monuments and inscriptions found elsewhere it contains an unsurpassed collection of graffiti scratched into its walls and pillars. The north wall under the tower bears some of the most historically interesting, recalling in harrowing words the horror of the Black Death that reached its height in the middle of the 14th century. Another records the terrible storm that swept across the country in

12

the middle of January 1361, causing widespread devastation.

This same wall also carries a highly detailed sketch of a large church, thought to be London's Gothic cathedral of St Paul's before it was re-faced by Inigo Jones in the 1630s, only to be completely destroyed by the Great Fire of London in 1666. This magnificent church was one of the great buildings of medieval Europe, longer than Wren's cathedral which succeeded it, longer too than Winchester Cathedral, now the longest cathedral in England. Its spire, destroyed by lightning in 1561, reached a height of 490 feet, and its east window, which forms much of the detailed graffiti at Ashwell, was a magnificent rose design that was much copied throughout the Middle Ages.

The identity of the draughtsman who scratched this design at Ashwell makes interesting speculation, but authorities agree that whoever he or she was, the graffiti must have been inscribed some time in the 14th or 15th centuries, after work began on the tower at Ashwell and before the collapse of the spire of St Paul's (if indeed the building shown is Old St Paul's; Westminster Abbey makes a rival, but less well substantiated, claim).

Other medieval drawings and writings appear on the pillars in the nave, including one that bemoans in Latin a wayward girl, *Barbara filia barbara est*. This is a neat pun written by an anguished lover or parent which translates as 'The daughter Barbara is a barbarian', though the adjective *barbara* has connations of uncouthness and even cruelty.

Whatever our feelings may be about the graffiti of our own day, the medieval 'vandals' of Ashwell have left us some intriguing pointers to the things that played on their minds and occupied them in their idle moments.

St Mary, Astbury, Cheshire

At the top of the little green at Astbury stands the battlemented church of St Mary, seemingly quite out of proportion with the size of the present village until one learns that, when it was built, St Mary's was the parish church of nearby Congleton.

A Saxon church is recorded at Astbury in the Domesday Book, but nothing of this remains except for a few pieces of carved stone. A Norman church followed on the site, but only for a comparatively short time before a larger Early English structure took its place. Today the lower part of the belfry tower and a number of carved sections of doorway are the sole surviving remnants of the Norman building.

The belfry tower stands apart from the main body of the church, linked only by a narrow passage. Over the centuries it became gradually isolated as the 13th-century builders and their 15th-century successors moved the nave progressively southwards from that of their Norman forebears. Three gargoyles on the belfry tower illustrate various aspects of human frailty and failing; Lust to the west, Deceit to the east and Lost Innocence to the north.

For the most part St Mary's is built in the Perpendicular style. The south side, topped with battlements, has tall *clerestory* windows in the upper storey of the nave, finely worked in durable millstone grit, a stone that is rare in

14

Cheshire but retains much of its clarity of detail in the decorated ribs of the window tracery.

In addition to the belfry tower there is the peel tower at the western end, the base of which forms the fine western porch through which one enters the church. Above the porch are two rooms formerly used as 'peels' or refuge rooms during periodic raids across the border from Wales. From here access can be gained to the almost flat roof of the nave, which gave those taking refuge freedom to move about and stretch their legs more than they would have been able to do in the cramped conditions of the interior of the tower.

Inside the porch are interesting details reminding the visitor of the ceremony of exorcism which all infants about to be baptized had once to undergo before entering the church proper. A carved skull and crossbones is depicted, reminding the congregation that 'In Adam all die'. Other carvings show angels playing musical instuments and a very angry devil displaying violent rage at the prospect of another soul about to be saved from his clutches by being baptized. When the exorcism was completed, the child was carried into the church, passing beneath a boss showing the dove symbolizing the Holy Spirit, the Lord and Giver of Life.

The southern entrance is adorned with another fine two-storey porch, above which is located the Priest's Room, entered by means of a staircase made from stone grave-covers.

Once inside the church, the woodwork for which Astbury is justly famous is immediately apparent. The Jacobean box pews are worth special study in themselves, for the majority of the panels are of different designs. The *rood screen* with its exquisite 15th-century fan tracery divides the nave from the chancel, for no chancel arch was built in the Perpendicular church. The choir stalls and screens separating the south chapel and the Moreton chapel (on the north side) display craftsmanship of the same superb delicacy and were carved at around the same date.

The lectern, carved in black oak, shows a stiffly formed eagle and comes from the early 16th century.

The beautiful font cover is also Jacobean; the font itself is medieval, but was much altered during the restoration of the church in 1862.

Above all else (quite literally) St Mary's glories in its roofs, almost entirely carved in the 15th century. In the chancel the pendant that hangs over the high altar is carved on its underside with the five wounds of Christ, and is just one example of the supreme artistry in which the carving at Astbury excels. Above the Lady chapel more than fifty horned devils look down from the roof, along with a fox preaching to a flock of geese (a pointed reference to the qualities of both the medieval incumbent and congregation by at least one of the craftsmen at work here). The fine hammer-beams that support the roof are hidden from view by the carved figures of angels holding shields that display the instruments of Christ's Passion among which are: the cup of vinegar, the nails, the dice, the crown of thorns, the crowing cock and the cross itself.

Pre-dating all of this work, however, is the venerable yew tree standing in the churchyard, which first poked its top above the ground over a thousand years ago when the earliest Christians in the area began to gather and worship at Astbury.

St Mark and St Luke, Avington, Berkshire

Berkshire has little Norman architecture and this small church, standing at the end of a short lane off the A4 among meadows watered by the River Kennet, is the only church in the county to retain its original Norman plan, with only the minor addition of a north vestry, built on the site of a 13th-century *chantry chapel*, and a south porch.

Avington church stands alone among trees, its buff rendered walls and mellow red-tiled roof blending with its surroundings. The west end, the first to be seen, is a simple gable with two round-headed apertures, one above the other. Both were originally windows, but the upper opening now has louvres because, since the Early English bell-cote was removed, the bell has hung in the gable.

The south porch was brought from the nearby Elizabethan manor house after that had burned to the ground in 1769. It carries the initials RC, which probably stand for Richard Choke who took up residence there in 1564.

The exterior of the church is plain and unembellished for the most part, the exception being the south door which still carries the rich zigzag moulding that formed part of its decoration.

Inside the church is dark and mysterious, with the small Norman windows set high in the walls. At the

17

western end there is a wide round wooden arch supporting the bell in the west gable.

The font is large, round and decorated with a relief
of eleven continuous arches in which lurk single figures or pairs of figures that remain to be accurately
identified. Pevsner described it as being 'exceptionally
interesting' and had a stab at interpreting some of the
figures before breaking off, presumably in some bewilder-
ment.

Complementing this is the chancel arch, which is also
elaborately decorated. This has outer courses of large and
small zigzag designs, inside which runs a course of carved
heads: beakheads on the east and monsters' and cats'
heads on the west, neither of which are commonly found
inside churches. The chancel arch is also distinctive in
shape, or rather the lack of it, brought about by the failure
of the crown at some time after its construction. This has
caused the arch to sag disconcertingly in the middle. A recess in the wall above it may have been created to relieve
weight on the arch, though a *rood* or *doom* may equally
have been housed here.

Evidence that the chancel may have been vaulted at
one time survives in the *corbels* around the walls and
traces of moulding that might have formed the ribs. In
the eastern end are corbels carved to show the heads of a
lion and an ox, the symbols respectively of St Mark and
St Luke; others of a similar nature may also have been
included when the chancel was first built. The chancel
also contains a small round-arched *piscina* in the south
wall and a wide round-arched *sedilia* sightly further to
the west. The *aumbry* in the north, where the sacred
vessels for mass would have been kept, is fitted with
doors designed by the famous Victorian architect and
church 'restorer', William Butterfield during his work on
the church in the last century. These repeat the pierced
trefoil decoration seen in the communion rails.

Butterfield was also responsible for the floor tiles in the chancel, though the grey and black stone diagonals set in the floor of the sanctuary are more likely to be part of the restoration carried out in the 18th century. With the addition of a few minor furnishings these, and the additions already mentioned, are the only appreciable changes that have taken place in this little church since it was first built by the River Kennet eight centuries ago.

St Nicholas, Barfreston, Kent

9 MILES NORTH-WEST OF DOVER, OFF A2

St Nicholas, Barfreston, is not only one of the finest Norman churches in southern England, it also possesses some of the most interesting and beautifully worked stone carving of the period. Why so small a parish church should have received craftsmanship of such high quality is uncertain, for it seems possible that craftsmen of the same 'school' as those who worked on the cathedrals at Rochester and Canterbury may have come to Barfreston some two decades after the Norman invasion to begin work on the church.

Whatever the reason for the quality of the work, St Nicholas's has benefited from it ever since. Small, compact and richly decorated, it provides a rewarding study of early medieval symbolism.

As with so many Norman churches, the south doorway at Barfreston contains some of the most elaborate and interesting carving. The *tympanum* (semi-circular stone above the door filling the upper part of the arch) shows Christ in majesty, giving a blessing with his right hand while holding open a book on his knee with his left. Surrounding the seated figure of Christ are tendrils of foliage that are woven to form enclosures within which sit members of the heavenly host, and rulers here on earth. The capitals on either side of the door are decorated with a stylized leaf (on the west) representing the Tree of Knowledge and the Tree of Life, and two tilting

20

The immense appeal of St Patrick, Patrington, lies in its uniformity of design and construction.

The magnificent spire of St Mary's, Bloxham, rises to 198 ft.

knights (on the east), symbols of justice through trial by combat.

Around the outside of the arch over the south door, immediately below the dripstone, are fourteen stones depicting various activities that once formed part of the yearly cycle in the manor house and estate. There are men-at-arms displaying their weapons, estate workers like the woodcutter trimming a piece of timber, the forester loosing off an arrow from his bow, the miller carrying his staff and bag of corn, and members of the household like the steward with his ledger, the minstrel with his instrument and the 'butler' drawing drink from a cask. Elijah, John the Baptist and King David also appear.

Inside this semicircle, but separated from it by a string of chevron moulding, are twelve more activities, recreational this time, carved on a half-round moulding. In the middle of them, at the top of the arch, sits a figure dressed like a bishop, thought to represent God the Father. On either side are scenes of dancing, drinking and partying in general represented for the most part by grotesques. There's an actor of sorts there, too, performing a mime. The other images show hunting scenes and include a curious representation of a monkey riding a goat and carrying a dead hare on its shoulder.

One final detail worth noting at this splendid south door is purely functional, but no less revealing. These are the scratch dials, or *mass dials*, on the flat faces of the door jambs which were used to show the hour when mass was said each day. The arrival of clocks late in the 13th century put an end to their use.

The east end presents the most richly ornate side of the church, divided into three distinct sections. In the topmost of these is a large wheel window divided into eight sections. Around this is a frieze that is decorated both inside the church and out with animals' heads and angels, entwined in a garland of foliage and flowers. At one time the figures of Christ and the four symbols of the evangelists were set in niches around this window, but only the eagle of St John survives today and now stands on the left of the window. In the northern niche is a badly weathered figure which may possibly have been the original figure of Christ. To the left of the window is a carving showing St Martin of Tours on horseback sharing his cloak with the beggar at Amiens; this was the image the barons of Dover had stamped as a motif on the reverse of their seal.

The middle section of the eastern end has four small arched recesses, between which are three narrow windows. The symbolic carving here shows a man in a long garment lying down with a lizard-like creature sniffing at his heels. Opposite this is a smiling human face, possibly representing the sun. According to medieval iconography the lizard lost its sight as it grew old and only regained it by hiding in an east-facing wall and sticking out its head to the rising sun, whose rays restored its sight. Interpreted as a moral of human life, this apparently shows how men can lose their spiritual blindness, but it looks as though it would need a pretty bright medieval peasant to work it out.

The lowest part of the eastern end consists of two depressed arched buttresses which physically support and visually balance the two upper sections.

Along the eaves running round the church are a series of carved *corbels* that may represent evil spirits driven from the church at the time of its consecration and put on show as a warning to others with ideas of slipping inside to cause mischief among the congregation.

The interior of St Nicholas's is as richly decorated as its exterior. The chancel arch is heavily moulded, leading the eye to the east end where the effect of the three narrow windows below the wheel window can be fully appreciated. On either side of the chancel arch are two smaller arched recesses with rich chevron moulding, which formerly housed the sub-altars of St Catherine on the south side and St Nicholas on the north.

A string course of grotesque human and other heads runs round just below the windows of the nave showing more extraordinary flights of creative imagination.

Above the windows in both nave and chancel are hood mouldings in bold dog-tooth designs.

The stained glass is mostly fairly modern and the church was considerably restored in the middle of the last century at a time when it was in danger of almost total collapse.

St Mary the Virgin, Battle, East Sussex

The town of Battle, its ruined abbey and the parish church all owe their existence to the vow made by William the Conqueror on 14 October 1066 that, if he defeated the English army led by King Harold, he would build a church on the site to commemorate his victory for ever. This he did, though nothing remains above ground of the building he erected. When the foundations were excavated the plan was easy to distinguish; the high altar was situated where King Harold fell and in 1903 a memorial stone to him was placed there to mark the spot.

Some time after William built his church, Benedictine monks established an abbey close by. As time passed a small community grew up around this, and the need arose for a chapel to serve the parishioners. The building constructed for this purpose was a small simple structure with an aisleless nave and a little chancel, built in about the year 1115. The priest placed in charge of the 'chapel in honour of the Blessed Mother of God' was given the style and title of Dean and the parish was designated as a Royal Peculiar, which removed it from the jurisdiction of the Bishop of Chichester in whose diocese it lay – a situation that lasted 730 years until 1845. The royal connection holds fast today, none the less, with the sovereign acting as patron and the incumbent bearing the title the Very Reverend the Dean of Battle.

24

Work on enlarging the church began towards the end of the 12th century. The monks built lean-to extensions to act as aisles, creating the late Romanesque nave that is one of the church's prime features. The square marble font decorated with a frieze of arches dates from the same century.

Alterations to the chancel began in about 1230 with its extension and almost total rebuilding in the Early English style; most of that still stands today (except the east wall, which has been altered and restored since that date).

The church's first tower was built on the site of St Catherine's chapel, at the east end of the south aisle, in the middle of the 12th century; the present tower was added in the middle of the 15th century at the same time as the north aisle. In St Catherine's chapel the emblem of the wheel on which she was martyred can be seen, as well as little crosses on the pillar behind the Dean's stall which are thought to have been inscribed by knights returning from crusades. The long scratched slits have also been attributed to them, marking places where they are said to have blunted their swords.

Restoration work on the paintings in St Mary's has revealed extensive work on the north and south walls of the nave and above the chancel arch. The north wall shows two dozen scenes from the life of St Margaret of Antioch, who was popularly associated with childbirth in the Middle Ages. Running from right to left in the top row and then left to right in the lower one, these have been dated to the period around the beginning of the 14th century.

In the middle part of that century the Lady chapel was built and between that and the high altar stands the richly decorated alabaster tomb of Henry VIII's Master of Horse, Sir Anthony Browne, and his wife, to whom Henry granted Battle Abbey and its estates in 1539. It was Sir Anthony who demolished many of the abbey buildings and turned the abbot's lodgings into a private house.

The Minster Church of St John the Evangelist, Beverley, Humberside

Capital of the former East Riding of Yorkshire, Beverley possesses in its minster one of the most beautiful Gothic churches in Europe. Today St John's is used as a parish church, although it has always been known as the minster and was served by a college of secular canons established back in the 10th century by King Athelstan.

It was to Beverley, where he had established an earlier monastery, that John, Bishop of Hexham and later of York, retired to end his days, and where he died in the year 721. It seems likely that his original monastery would have been destroyed in the Viking invasions in the centuries that followed. But his memory and growing reputation as a worker of miracles lived on. Confirmation of the veneration of, and devotion to him came in 1037 when he was canonized as St John of Beverley, and the splendid medieval church that grew here over the centuries is his lasting memorial, although the monastery has long since disappeared.

Disasters befell the earlier Norman church as well. First came a catastrophic fire that swept through the town in 1188 to be followed, less than half a century later, by the collapse of the central tower during ambitious rebuilding.

However, these setbacks left the way clear for the

building of the present church which began in the first half of the 13th century with the exquisite Early English choir, transepts and now vanished chapter house. This work is characterized by the pointed arches of the period, the *lancet* windows and deeply-cut mouldings. Elegant clustered shafts of dark Purbeck marble counterpoint the pristine simplicty of limestone walls, and add a delicacy and refinement to the work as it broke away from the stolid influences of the Norman period that had gone before.

Following the completion of the eastern end of the church, attention turned to reconstructing the nave. Funds were raised nationally to cover the work and the completion of a gorgeous gold and silver shrine to St John of Beverley helped swell the coffers of the building fund as pilgrims came in increasing numbers in search of comfort or practical medical aid in the form of a miracle of two.

A large part of the nave was built in the first half of the 14th century and, though designed in the Decorated style, it harmonizes delicately with the Early English work at the eastern end from the century before.

The last major undertaking, which embraced the west end of the nave with its two beautiful towers and the wonderful north porch, belongs to the Perpendicular style and dates from the decades straddling the turn of the 15th century. At the same time the great east window was constructed and this today houses what remains of the minster's medieval glass.

These, then, were the principal phases in the erection of this magnificent church. Decoration and embellishment followed in successive centuries and right into the present, but the essential fabric of the church has retained its integrity since the high Middle Ages.

Beverley Minster has three towers, though one would be forgiven for failing to notice the squat one in the centre so compellingly outshone by the two western towers. Although individually these are probably rather thin for their height, they were conceived as an ensemble and together achieve an effortless impression of soaring grace. The towers at Beverley are unusual, too, for their rectangular plan which permits two median pinnacles on the east and west sides as against only one on the north and south sides – a design that again is in perfect harmony with the overall plan of the church.

Before going inside, the 'highgate' or north porch must be seen for its superb panelled façade, enhanced by the addition in the niches of modern figures replacing the original ones that were no doubt destroyed in the reformation. One other detail worth noting is the unusual plan of the minster: it is shaped as a double cruciform.

To complement its magnificent exterior, the Minster of St John the Evangelist has several notable internal features that rank in the forefront of European medieval art. First among these is the widely acclaimed Percy Tomb, north of the sanctuary, regarded as the finest 14th-century example of its kind. Enshrining the wife of either the first or second Lord Percy of Alnwick, this glorious tomb has a canopy of exquisitely worked carving of fruit and foliage, animals and angels which blends perfectly with the slightly later *reredos* close by.

In its choir Beverley has sixty-eight superb 16th-century stalls with the largest collection of *misericords*, or seats of mercy, in the country. These provided a degree of support for the clergy during the long hours they spent standing at their divine offices. Many are very fine examples of medieval carving.

Among the oldest fittings in the church is the 12th-century font, a huge Norman affair cut from Frosterley marble; it is decorated with simple arcading and supported by a multiple stem with clawed feet. The ornate font cover dating from 1726 is thought to have been designed by the architect Nicholas Hawksmoor, who worked under both Wren and Vanbrugh. During his restoration work the great west door was embellished with the panels bearing carved figures of the four evangelists, John, Luke, Mark and Matthew (in order from left to right) together with their symbols.

In addition to its aesthetic attractions, the minster has a number of unusual features well worth seeing. Up in the squat central tower there's a giant treadmill, very similar to the small ones that pet mice race around in. This is still in use today for lifting or lowering building materials through a hole in the ceiling disguised by a movable boss.

Close to the Percy Tomb stands a solid stone seat variously known as a 'frith stool' or 'sanctuary chair'. This dates from before the Norman Conquest and recalls the ancient rights of sanctuary that fugitives could claim before Henry VIII abolished most of those rights in 1540. The chair was probably the official seat occupied by the investigator appointed to examine pleas for asylum. Two types of sanctuary could be applied for: Outer Sanctuary, which could be claimed within the boundary marked by posts still standing in surrounding fields and by the roadside, and Full Sanctuary which could only be claimed by those inside the minster itself. In the last sixty years of its existence the right of sanctuary was claimed by well over 450 fugitives, and there are still Beverley families who can trace ancestors who made use of this privilege hundreds of years ago.

All Saints, Bisham, Berkshire

In spite of the extensive restoration that this 12th-century church underwent in the 19th century, its setting beside one of Berkshire's loveliest reaches of the Thames still makes All Saints a delightful church to visit, and one that contains a justifiably celebrated collection of monuments of the Hoby (pronounced *hobby*) family.

Bisham Abbey passed to the Hobys after the Dissolution when Sir Philip Hoby was serving as an ambassador on the Continent. In 1557 he had started building a house at Bisham and, following his death in 1566, his body was brought by water to Bisham to be buried in the church near his country seat.

Sir Thomas Hoby, half-brother to Sir Philip and twenty-five years his junior, took to the diplomatic life as well and flourished, if only for a brief period. He died while serving in Paris when he was only thirty-six, though not before he had taken to wife the resourceful if somewhat morbid Elizabeth Cooke.

Finding herself a widow, she began building a chapel to accommodate the tombs of the two Hoby brothers, composing epitaphs for them in English and Latin and installing a monument that has few equals among 16th-century memorials in this country. Both knights are shown lying in full and wonderfully detailed armour, their heads propped on their helmets.

Eight years later, however, she put away her widow's weeds and married Lord Russell, whose wife she remained for eleven years until he too died, obliging her once again to put pen to paper in composing another epitaph, destined this time for Westminster Abbey.

Lady Elizabeth herself lived on into her eighties, which allowed her plenty of time to plan and design her own obsequies and memorial. This is a magnificent creation which shows her effigy kneeling at a prayer desk, wearing a coronet. Facing her outside the canopy is Anne Russell, her only surviving daughter. Behind her kneel Elizabeth Russell, and Elizabeth and Anne Hoby – who all died before their mother. The same fate awaited poor little Thomas Russell, who died as a baby and is shown lying at his mother's feet. Outside the arch to the west are the two sons who did survive her, Sir Edward Hoby and Sir Thomas Posthumus Hoby (so named since he was born after his father's death).

For a woman who was so evidently preoccupied by death when she was alive, it seems only right that she should be equally concerned with life when dead. For Lady Hoby's ghost is not unknown at Bisham, where she has been seen vainly trying to clean her hands, like Lady Macbeth, in a bowl that is constantly eluding her. It is said that she is trying to remove the bloodstains of her son, whom she is accused of beating to death because of his careless blotting of his copy books. Weight was added to the legend during the 19th century when workmen carrying out some repairs came across a number of old exercise books, all of which were terribly blotchy and ink-stained. As Edith Sitwell commented in *English Eccentrics*, her appearance during her lifetime must have been every bit as alarming as her ghost is now. 'She was, when living, a pest of outstanding quality.'

31

The other Hoby monument of great interest is that erected by Lady Elizabeth's eldest son, Edward, in memory of his wife Margaret Carey. This stands before the church's famous armorial window and consists of an obelisk surmounted by a flaming heart at the base of which are four swans, the family emblem of the Careys.

St Mary, Bloxham, Oxfordshire

3 MILES SOUTH-WEST OF BANBURY, ON A361

Bloxham is a largish village rising on either side of a valley topped on one side by its public school and on the other by its outstanding parish church, with a magnificent spire 198 feet high.

The church is built of the local limestone, which is particularly suited to the construction of spires; the neighbouring churches of Adderbury and King's Sutton are equally well endowed with fine spires of their own.

Previous Saxon and Norman churches probably stood on the site of the present church, and traces of late-Norman work can be seen in the south doorway and chancel arch. However, the majority of the church is 13th century, enlarged and improved in the two centuries that followed.

The 13th-century builders were able to incorporate Norman beak and cable mouldings into the east window of the north wall of the chancel and all the windows in its south wall; the chancel also has a fine Norman door in the north wall that now leads into the vestry. The chancel screen, 15th century in origin, retains the original figure paintings on its panels and the rest of it has been repainted in what are believed to have been the original colours.

The north side of the nave has solid columns recalling those of the Norman period, while the south side has lovely clustered pillars, two of which have capitals carved with the stiff-leaf moulding that typified Early English decoration.

Later in the 13th century, early in the Decorated period of church construction, the north aisle and north transept were built. Separating the two is the striking diamond-shaped pillar supporting two arches which is one of the principal points of interest in the church. Its capital is elaborately carved with figures with linked arms. One of those depicted is thought to be St George, who holds his shield in his left hand and his banner in his right, both bearing his familiar emblem.

The windows at the west end of the north aisle are 14th century and that in the west wall shows Christ in the centre of the wheel-shaped tracery surrounded by the symbols of the four evangelists.

The south aisle was also rebuilt early in the 14th century, though the eastern end was later altered. The western window has finely worked tracery of double triangles.

Outside the church, the south porch and doorway are further evidence of the way in which St Mary's evolved over the centuries. There are 'recycled' Norman zigzag mouldings on the outside arch, and stone steps lead up to the lower of two priest's rooms. This one was built in the 13th century at the same time as the porch and doorway, and still retains its fireplace.

The upper priest's room was built in the 15th century at the same time as the Milcombe chapel, the east windows at the ends of both aisles and the *clerestory* of the nave. The quality of the masonry in the Milcombe chapel is widely praised and gives rise to the possibility that it may have been the work of Richard Winchcombe, who was master mason during the construction of the Divinity School at Oxford around 1430. The figures in the *reredos* were carved at the end of the last century, and the stone altar was restored during the general restoration of the church carried out by G.E. Street in the 1860s. In all other respects, though, the Milcombe chapel is a supreme example of the mason's skill and innovation in the Perpendicular period.

The tower and steeple were erected late in the 14th century, with massive buttresses rising to the four pinnacles attached to the *hollis* or stone gallery. The west door is decorated with mouldings in a pattern of foliage, flowers, birds and cones, and around the *hood-mould* above it sit the twelve Apostles. Above them is a well-preserved representation of the Last Judgement providing a centrepiece for this handsome tower and steeple that act as a splendid landmark beckoning visitors to this magnificent church.

St Mary and St Martin, Blyth, Nottinghamshire

The church of St Mary and St Martin stands to the north of the triangular village green, as it has done since the end of the 11th century when it was first constructed as the priory church of the Benedictine monastery that flourished in Blyth until 1535.

In the nave and north aisle the church preserves one of the earliest examples of Norman architecture in the country, heavy, austere and uncompromising. When first built the church would have had an *apse* and north and south transepts. The Early English *groined roof* was added to the nave at the beginning of the 13th century, towards the end of which the south aisle was widened to its present dimensions. From the next century comes the well-proportioned tower, and late in the 14th century it's believed that a dispute between the parishioners and the monks led to the building, at the east end of the nave, of a wall which was then decorated with the painting of the Last Judgement, one of the best remaining in the country.

The Dissolution of the Monasteries brought an end to the priory. The monastic buildings, including the part of the church which belonged to the priory, east of the new wall, were demolished and the materials used for other buildings in the village, in particular Blyth Hall, the great house that stood to the north of the church until 1972, when it too was taken down. The hall was home to the Mellish family for two hundred years until they moved to their other property at Hodsock, just down the road, and there are many memorials to members of the family in the church.

Holy Trinity, Blythburgh, Suffolk

Except for the magnificent sight of Holy Trinity rising from the marshy estuary as you approach Blythburgh along the London to Lowestoft road, there is little today to suggest that this was one of the busiest medieval ports on the east coast.

In the mid-15th century Blythburgh's wharves were lined with ships from home and abroad, twice a year its streets were given over to Charter fairs and the town boasted its own mint and gaol. On the spiritual level, Henry I had founded a priory here and, three hundred or so years later, in 1412, the prior settled on the plan of building Holy Trinity as a fitting symbol and affirmation of this prosperity. A royal licence was granted for a new parish church and building work began, incorporating the tower of the earlier church into the splendid new structure.

For eighty years the work progressed. Parish records show legacies and bequests from well-to-do townspeople. Even before the century was out, however, the tide of trade that had raised the town's fortunes began to ebb. Larger ships with deeper draughts were brought into service. Blythburgh, lying at the head of shallow river channels, was no longer accessible from the sea. The wealth of the townspeople and of their church begin to wane: '16d and no more because the Bretons did not come this year with salt', laments the entry in the parish records for 1478.

Fifty years later Holy Trinity suffered a further blow when the Pope granted Cardinal Wolsey permission to suppress the priory at Blythburgh along with a number of similar small religious establishments. Wolsey's express intention had been to found a college at Ipswich. This never materialized, however, and, with the priory deserted and decaying, Holy Trinity was no longer able to rely on the protection of erstwhile benevolent neighbours.

In 1577, according to local tradition, the devil added to the church's misfortunes when he arrived on Sunday 4 August with 'a strange and terrible tempest' that struck the church so violently that the steeple was sent smashing through the roof, seriously damaging the font and killing two of the congregation. The north door still bears the scorch marks said to have been left by the devil as he rushed out in the direction of Bungay. The date carved on the cross-beam shows that the roof was not fully repaired until 1782, and the toppled steeple was never rebuilt.

The most lasting and evident damage to this fine old church came at the hand of man, and of one man in particular, the Puritan zealot, William Dowsing. He arrived with a band of followers on 8 April 1644 and set about the wholesale destruction of the church's treasures. Memorial brasses were torn from tombs. Horses were tethered in the nave (remains of tethering rings can still be seen in the pillars). Statues were destroyed. Even Holy Trinity's famed tie-beam roof could not escape. Since it was far above their reach, Dowsing's troops fired hundreds of shots at its wooden angels, shattering their wings and peppering the brightly painted medieval timbers with shot.

When Dowsing and his men rode out of Blythburgh, they left a scene of desolation that remained crudely patched up for over two centuries. It is only within the last hundred years that steps have been taken to restore Holy Trinity to something like its medieval glory.

In 1954 American benefactors donated the unpainted angels' wings to replace those destroyed by Dowsing and his followers. Twenty years earlier minor reinforcement was made to the roof, which, apart from repairs made after the steeple crashed through, had remained untouched for five hundred years.

Similar displays of the woodcarver's skill can be seen in the elegantly worked bench-ends that make up the series of the Seven Deadly Sins. Finely worked finials like these are known as *poppy-heads*, a name that comes from the Latin word *puppis*, meaning the figurehead of a ship. Gluttony sits holding his bloated stomach, Drunkenness languishes in the stocks, Avarice sits on a money chest. Their fellow 'sins' are gathered nearby in familiar attitudes. Elsewhere you find the four seasons: Spring going forth to sow, Summer binding a sheaf of hay, Autumn reaping and Winter killing his pig for the lean months ahead.

Apostles and saints appear in the carvings on the frontals of the choir stalls, the figures most likely coming originally from a *rood loft* no longer in existence, although the stair by which it was approached is still there by the entrance door in the north wall. At one time the choir-stalls stood in the Hopton chantry when it served as a schoolroom. Deep holes in the book-rests show where inkwells were once held, and one pupil resorted to the book-rest itself to leave a more permanent reminder of his education – in 1665 Dirck Lowersen from Stockholm passed his time by carving his name so deeply that we can still read it today.

The lectern dates from the mid-15th century and, in spite of the ravages of woodworm, remains a fine example of medieval carving. The story of two robins is recorded in the embroidery of the lectern cover. One made her nest in the lectern early in the 1880s and successfully hatched her eggs. The second nested in the same place half a century later, in 1931. Both are also remembered in the church-wardens' staffs that are topped by little brass robins.

Holy Trinity, Blythburgh is also one of the few churches to retain a Jack-o'-The-Clock, the painted wooden figure of a man dressed in armour which originally struck the hours of the clock. Today he stops the ringing of the bell and announces the entry of the clergy at the beginning of each service.

The font, so badly damaged when the steeple fell in 1577, is a 'seven sacrament' font from the 15th century. Octagonal in shape, it was originally made with eight panels; seven depicted the sacraments of baptism, confirmation, mass, penance, extreme unction, ordination and matrimony, and the eight another subject of unknown identity. In the course of restoration work, the panels have had to be covered over with plain inset ones that act as reinforcement.

As a final reminder of the men who built this magnificent old church, keep an eye out for mason's marks. There are several to be found about the church pillars, three on the one standing behind the pulpit.

Holy Trinity, Bosham, West Sussex

Few churches in England can have associations with pre-Conquest kings of England as well documented as those of Holy Trinity, Bosham, to which both Canute and the ill-fated Harold came to worship.

Lying beside a tidal creek, Bosham has been a safe haven for small craft since ancient times. This was one of the first sites on the south coast permanently settled by the Romans and the bases of the chancel arch are believed to be the remains of Roman columns that could well have supported a basilica on the same site.

Bede refers to a small Irish monastery based in Bosham before the arrival of St Wilfrid and his missionary work in the 7th century. However, history falls silent for the next three centuries and leaves the field open to speculation, albeit speculation based on reasonably sound proof. This is where King Canute enters the story of Holy Trinity.

With the tower, nave and part of the chancel dating from Saxon times, it's reasonable to imagine that they may have been erected during the reign of Canute which began in 1017. He instigated a lot of repair work to churches damaged during the Danish raids that preceded his succession; Bosham could have been one of the churches to benefit. Furthermore, there is a long-held belief that Canute had an official residence at Bosham and may well have performed the most memorable event of his reign here, namely demonstrating his inability to

42

turn back the tide. (Southampton makes a similar claim, of course.)

However, Canute does have a rather more substantial link with the Bosham church, based on the belief that he buried his youngest daughter in Holy Trinity after her death at the age of eight. In 1865 a stone coffin was uncovered beneath the floor; it dated from the period in which Canute ruled and contained the bones of a child of about his daughter's age.

In 1064 the future King Harold embarked at Bosham on his fateful voyage to meet Duke William of Normandy. The Bayeux Tapestry, no less, records his visit to the church, showing Harold and one of his followers entering a building that, it has to be said, bears scant resemblance to Holy Trinity as Harold would have seen it. That it is Bosham church there can be no doubt, as the Latin commentary states, *'Ubi Harold Dux Anglorum et sui milites equitant ad Bosham: ecclesia.'* ('Where Harold King of the English and his soldiers rode to Bosham: church.')

High in the north wall of the nave three small circular windows are a further reminder of the defensive as well as pastoral role played by Saxon churches around the coast of England. These windows are so positioned as to minimize the risk to anyone sheltering inside from the arrows or stones of marauders from the sea. The tower arch and the triangular-headed opening above are good examples of Saxon long-and-short work, so called because alternate long and short stones are placed above one another. The tower is mainly Saxon in construction, too, and still retains one of the original Saxon windows with a well-preserved central baluster.

The nave arcades were built during the transitional period between Norman and Early English work. In the south aisle is an unusual 13th-century crypt that stands about five feet above the nave floor and sinks the same

depth below it. It has a fine *groined roof,* and was probably used as a charnel house for the bones of deceased
members of the college of secular canons based here in
the Middle Ages. At the eastern end of the south aisle
the early 13th-century font stands on a central column
surrounded by four smaller shafts.

The chancel at Bosham is one third Early English, one
third Norman and one third Saxon, beginning with the
Saxon chancel arch, regarded as one of the best examples
in the country. This is described as 'horseshoe'-shaped,
being wider above than below. The capitals are interesting, consisting of a large square stone on top of a round
one, reversing the pattern of the bases below.

Further up the chancel, the window that now opens
into the vestry and the remains of the *piscina* in the
south wall are all that remain of the Norman work.
The rest is Early English, culminating in the impressive
five-light east window.

From the 14th century comes the south porch with its
original nail-studded door on the inside. At one time the
door apparently carried a portion of a Dane's skin, flayed
from a captured raider by the Saxon forefathers of Bosham
and fastened to the church door as a sign that the captive
had been guilty of sacrilege.

Slightly less gruesome reminders of the past are the
small crosses scratched on the stonework of the door
which may have been inscribed by the sword-points of
crusaders returning home and visiting Holy Trinity as
the first church encountered after landing on home soil.

St Mary the Virgin, Bottesford, Leicestershire

Bottesford Church, also known as the 'Lady of the Vale', is indissolubly linked with the history of nearby Belvoir Castle. For this fine parish church with its lovely spire is where the lords of Rutland were laid to rest in great style for three hundred years, between the Reformation and the early 19th century, alongside medieval memorials which were brought to Bottesford after the dissolution of Belvoir Priory and Croxton Abbey where their forebears had been originally buried.

Over the great west door are the arms of Robert de Roos, Lord of Belvoir in the 13th century, who founded the present church. His effigy – which stands on the north wall of the chancel, just inside the altar rail – is the oldest monument in the church. It is also one of the most modest, for the Belvoir tombs present a fascinating study of changing aristocratic taste and self-confidence, with the result that one monument blocks the view of the altar from the nave and together with the others makes movement within the chancel particularly tricky for lengthy processions.

Robert de Roos is represented twice, and slightly further down the north wall of the chancel is another effigy or heart stone, bearing an inscription that explains that while his body was buried at Kirkham in Yorkshire,

45

where he died, his heart was brought back to Croxton Abbey (later to be transferred to Bottesford). The practice of burying the heart of an important man separately was common practice in the Middle Ages.

Styles of dress and armour from various periods are well represented in the carving of many of the tombs. Those on either side of the high altar show William de Roos and his son John, Lord Roos, who both died in the first quarter of the 15th century and are shown wearing armour. Both of these tombs were moved to the church from Belvoir Priory.

The first of these burials to take place in the church was that of Thomas Manners, First Earl of Rutland, who died in 1543. He won the favour of Henry VIII in assisting the king with the divorce of his wife, Catherine of Aragon, and was equally pragmatic in the help he gave the Duke of Norfolk in brutally suppressing the revolt of the Catholics in the north.

In the centre of the chancel stands the extraordinary tomb of the second earl and his wife, who are shown lying beneath a highly decorated Elizabethan dining-table. On top of the table are the kneeling figures of their three children.

The tombs of the third and fourth earls were created at the same time, for only ten months separated their deaths. The fourth earl is shown wearing less armour than his elder brother, marking a move to a more civilian style of representation. Six of his nine children are shown on the tomb as well; there were seven effigies originally, but one has since disappeared.

The richest tomb is that of the fifth earl, who endowed the white almshouse opposite the church in 1612.

The most mysterious is the so-called Witchcraft Tomb, which is unique in recording the deaths by witchcraft of two heirs to an earldom. The unfortunate victims were the infant sons of Francis, Sixth Earl of Rutland, as well as his two wives Frances and Cecilia. Cecilia gave birth to the two little boys 'both who died in their infancy by wicked practice and sorcerye'. The witches held responsible for their deaths were three local women, Joan Flower and her two daughters Margaret and Ruth. All three worked at Belvoir and developed a malicious grudge against the family after Margaret had been dismissed for stealing. With a series of increasingly powerful spells it seems they afflicted first the parents and finally the children. Only Katherine, the daughter by the earl's first marriage, survived. In the winter of 1617 the three supposed witches were arrested together with three 'accomplices'. Joan Flower attempted to prove her innocence by eating bread and butter; it seems she died in the process, which apparently confirmed her guilt. Her two daughters subsequently confessed at their trial and were hanged in March 1618.

The tombs of the seventh and eighth earls date from the middle of the sixteenth century and are the work of Grinling Gibbons.

Later Belvoir burials were either transferred to or took place in the family mausoleum built at Belvoir Castle in 1828.

In addition to what is probably the finest collection of tombs in any English parish church, St Mary's possesses a finely worked Jacobean pulpit and a brass eagle lectern which again surpasses most of those seen in similar churches.

As you leave, take another look at the spire. It's 210 feet high yet, in 1610, a young steeplejack climbed to the top using the *crockets* (leaf-shaped projer ions) as foot- and hand-holds, took down the weather-vane to repair a damaged portion, and then climbed back up again to replace it. He did this job for the princely sum of three shillings and sixpence!

Holy Trinity, Bottisham, Cambridgeshire

Bottisham is one of the best medieval churches in Cambridgeshire, with one of the finest Early English towers in the region. The chancel, too, dates from the 13th century but the rest of the church has remained structurally more or less unaltered since major rebuilding work carried out in the 14th century. Thus, unlike so many churches, it is possible to see at Bottisham a whole building designed and constructed in one constant progression. Not that this removes the anomalies that seem to be part and parcel of churches everywhere. At Bottisham a question mark hangs over the west porch.

This was clearly built as part of the 13th-century tower, but the purpose for which it was intended remains undecided. Today the porch is divided into two storeys. If this was always the case, then it is possible that the upper storey was intended to provide accommodation for a hermit. At a later stage it might also have given the parish priest somewhere to live.

The fine tower is built of a hard chalk known as *clunch* with *quoins* (dressed stones at the angles) made of the more durable Barnack stone. Sixty-six feet high, it has fine, widely splayed *lancet* windows.

The chancel is essentially a 13th-century structure as well. Its roof was originally more steeply pitched and the

48

four windows in the north and south date from the 15th century, but the *sedilia* where the clergy once sat and the double *piscina* are all Early English features. On the north side of the sanctuary is an Elizabethan communion table which replaced the medieval altar during that period. When it was in use this would have been placed in the centre of the chancel and would have been quite a bit longer than it is now; like so many others it was cut down, probably during the 18th century, when it was no longer needed for its original purpose.

The nave was built at the beginning of the Decorated period, spanning a couple of decades from about 1300 to 1320. It seems probable that it was conceived and funded by Elias de Beckingham, who lived in Bottisham and who was distinguished as being one of the 'just judges' of Edward I. There is an indentation for what must have been a very sumptuous brass memorial to him in the nave.

The stone chancel screen dates from the last quarter of the 15th century and is associated with Sir William Allington, a former Speaker of the House of Commons, whose table-tomb is by the pulpit. At one time this was covered by an elaborate canopy, and the arch above it may have been filled in at one time in order to create a *chantry chapel* to St Mary and St Martin, which would have been established to pray for Sir William in the life hereafter.

The five burials in the arches of the south wall of the south aisle are interesting too. These have governed the position of the nave windows and probably pre-date the nave, but whose graves they are remains a mystery.

St George, Brailes, Warwickshire

12 MILES SOUTH-EAST OF STRATFORD-UPON-AVON, ON B4035

St George's Church is the most striking reminder of the importance that Brailes enjoyed in the Middle Ages, when it was second only to Coventry and Warwick among the principal towns of Warwickshire, at a time when Birmingham was little more than a village.

By the 14th century Brailes had become an important market town with a thriving wool trade. As with many similar towns up and down the country, the time seemed right to celebrate this growing prosperity by rebuilding and enlarging the parish church and much of the present building dates from that period.

As the 'Cathedral of Feldon' (the rolling arable lands south of the Avon), St George's is stately in its proportions: the nave is over 150 feet long and the Perpendicular west tower stands 110 feet high. To the 14th century belong the extended nave, the *clerestory*, the new roof, the chancel with its magnificent east window and several external features: the openwork parapet on the south aisle, the carvings of animals' heads, grotesques and other decorations on the south side of the nave and the *crocketed* pinnacles.

In the following century St George's was given its splendid tower and the handsome square south porch. There are scratch marks in the masonry to the west of the window on the left which may have been made by archers sharpening their arrows at the time when archery

50

was regularly practised in churchyards as an important contribution to national defence.

Unfortunately it was fighting in the Civil War that probably caused considerable damage to St George's. Edgehill, the site of the first major engagement on 23 October 1642, is only a few miles away to the north and Royalist soldiers were quartered in Brailes during 1643, placing the town and church in the centre of the early campaigns and going some way to explaining why extensive rebuilding work had to take place in 1649, once the war had ended. This restoration under the Commonwealth might have provided an interesting rarity had it not been 'restored' itself in the 19th century.

One positive benefit of the 1879 restoration work was that it did reveal many of the original roof *corbels* that had been reversed or plastered over by the Commonwealth workmen. The organ was also installed in 1879.

Early in the 18th century the clock and carillon were both added to the church. These are electrically driven now and, using the church's six bells, the carillon plays four hymn tunes at set times throughout the day, with a different tune for Sundays.

The font in St George's, as in many churches, is one of the oldest features of the church. The one at Brailes was made in the 14th century, though the base is later and the cover added in 1879.

The fine framed oak chest with an intricately carved front dates from the 15th century. And if you want a test of patience to admire, look at the matchstick model of the church which took six years to complete and used an estimated quarter of a million matchsticks. This was placed in the church in 1979 to help raise funds for its upkeep.

St Brandon, Brancepeth, County Durham

St Brandon's at Brancepeth is celebrated for its collection of 'Cosin style' woodwork, named after John Cosin who was Rector of Brancepeth from 1626 and later became Bishop of Durham. Cosin undertook the restoration of many parish churches after the Commonwealth period and at Brancepeth he engaged Robert Barker to carve the pulpit, pews, screen, choir-stalls, roof and font cover.

St Brandon's stands in the grounds of Brancepeth castle. Both date from the 12th century, though the castle was subject to a considerable amount of Victorian rebuilding. The oldest part of the church is the 12th-century tower, with other portions being amended and added over the succeeding centuries. The 14th century showed the greatest changes: the tower was enclosed by the widening and extension of the aisles, the nave was extended and, later in the century, the chancel was built along with the chapel to the south of it and the Cosin Room to the north.

John Cosin erected the large wooden plaque on the north wall for his own memorial, but when he was elevated to the see of Durham this became redundant at Brancepeth; when the celebrated bishop died he was buried with an even more splendid memorial in the Bishop's Castle at Auckland.

'The naked rafters intricately crossed' that William Wordsworth admired in St Oswald's, Grasmere, were the solution to an enlargement problem caused by a growing congregation in sixteenth-century Cumbria.

All Saints, Brixworth, one of the oldest Saxon churches, was designed by monks from Peterborough, who followed the Roman basilica design.

The interior of St James, Louth - a Gothic masterpiece.

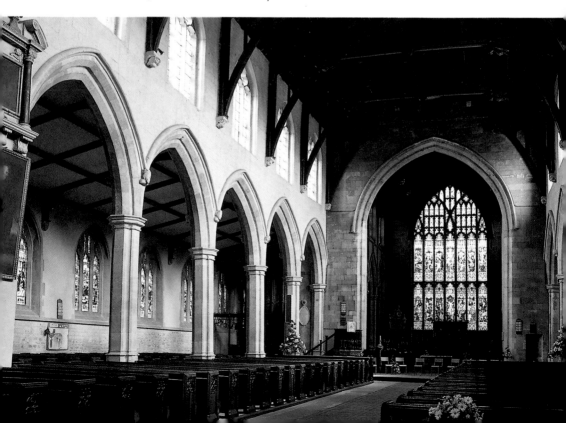

The style of interior decoration that Cosin brought to his churches is undeniably impressive, if something of a hybrid. Pevsner calls it 'One of the most remarkable contributions' made by County Durham to English architecture, and Alec Clifton-Taylor, writing in *English Parish Churches As Works of Art*, comments that it is 'stylistically something of a hotchpotch, and not exactly beautiful, but none the less a great enrichment to the churches that possess it'.

Cosin was Rector of Brancepeth in the early years of the reign of Charles I and the carvings and fittings here are essentially Jacobean in style, particularly the elaborate two-decker pulpit lavishly decorated with its little obelisks. However, the carving in the church also shows a conscious imitation of the medieval Gothic style, which contributes to its distinctive appearance.

In addition to the Cosin work, St Brandon's has a couple of interesting pieces of panelling over the chancel arch. The upper piece is a remnant of an old *rood loft* that shows the instruments of Christ's Passion in the centre row of symbols. The lower portion, with its intricately carved geometric patterns, may also be part of a former *rood screen*, though it could equally have been part of the old Jesus altar from Durham Cathedral, saved and brought to Brancepeth at the time of the Commonwealth.

In the Lady chapel of St Brandon's is an example of the work of a famous wood-carver from this century, Robert Thompson of Kilburn, who was nicknamed 'the mouse man' after the litle carved mouse with which he 'signed' his work. It was he who restored the fine 14th-century chest and converted it into an altar. You'll find his mouse on the north side of the altar.

St Helen, Brant Broughton, Lincolnshire

For all the insensitive – and to our eyes unfortunate – restoration undertaken by Victorian enthusiasts for medieval churches, it is reassuring to find in this lovely Lincolnshire church an example of Victorian work that is totally in harmony with that of the original builders back in the Middle Ages.

The success of this lies principally with Frederick and Arthur Sutton, uncle and nephew who were Rectors of Brant Broughton from 1873 until 1924. They matched generosity with learning and Frederick, in partnership with the architect G.F. Bodley, set about a wholesale refurbishment of the church which in spite of its obvious medieval attractions had been allowed to fall, in Canon Sutton's words, into a state of 'poverty and squalor'.

Bodley paid particular attention to the 15th-century angel roof, retaining as much of the original timber as he could along with most of the carvings; in the repainting he was just as careful to match the medieval colouring.

In the course of his work remains of a former Saxon church were found, but the building to which he devoted his attention belonged to the Perpendicular and Decorated periods of several centuries later.

The only exception to this was the chancel. The one Canon Sutton found at St Helen's was a poor structure built in 1812. This he had taken down, to be replaced with a completely new, perfectly proportioned, Gothic one. In 1887 Sutton installed the *reredos* behind the altar, complete with the late 15th-century panel of the Ascension which was painted by the German artist known as the Master of Leisborn. The influence of German work is carried through the whole *reredos*, which Sutton designed himself.

Canon Sutton also designed most of the stained glass in the church's ample supply of windows. He made a good deal of it, too, with some assistance, working with a kiln in the rectory garden. Not that he was any amateur. Thirty years earlier Sutton and his brother Augustus had tackled the west window, along with some of the other glass, in Lincoln cathedral.

The wrought-iron chandeliers, the chancel gates and those at the north entrance were made in the forge in the High Street worked by Messrs F. Coldon & Son, again to designs produced by the inventive incumbent. In 1890 his nephew and successor, Arthur Sutton, erected the *rood screen* and choir-stalls in his uncle's memory and in recognition of the invaluable work he had done in preserving St Helen's.

When it came to tackling the west window and tower vaulting, Bodley set about a reconstruction as close to the original designs as he was able to achieve and when Brant Broughton came to celebrate Queen Victoria's Diamond Jubilee in 1897, the opportunity presented itself to raise the height of the spire by seven feet to just short of 200 feet, which in Bodley's opinion was closer to its original height. To crown the zenith of this achievement a weather-vane was commissioned from the Coldrons and is still in its place at the pinnacle of this distinctive local landmark.

St Mary, Breamore, Hampshire

Standing beside noble cedars close to the red-brick Elizabethan manor house, Breamore church is one of the very few almost complete Saxon churches in Hampshire. Although little is known of its early history, a Saxon inscription in the south tower arch, which reads in translation 'Here the Covenant becomes manifest to Thee', suggests from the formation of some of the letters that the church was built during the reigns of Ethelred and Canute, around the year 980. From 1130 until the Reformation St Mary's was incorporated into an Augustinian priory, after the suppression of which it became a parish church once again.

When it was first built the church was essentially cruciform in shape with an aisleless nave, a square central tower off which ran a couple of modest transepts, and a chancel. (The north transept is no longer standing, thus altering the original plan of the building.)

Today the walls can be seen to be built of whole flints with large *quoins* of typical Saxon long-and-short work (see page 43), with *pilaster* strips of green sandstone and ironstone. Here again, its present appearance is at odds with the way it would have looked to Saxon congregations, as the walls both inside and out would have originally been covered with plaster, with only the quoins and pilasters remaining exposed.

In terms of the advance of church architecture,
Breamore represents an interesting evolution in the
development of the true cruciform design which became
such a prominent feature of medieval church building.
Whereas earlier Saxon churches had been built with side
chapels that projected from the nave, at Breamore the
quoins of the tower (which is the same width as the nave)
are carried right down to the ground. Inside the church
there is a square space between the nave and chancel
on either side of which narrow archways lead into side
chapels. These aren't transepts in the true sense because
they have lower roofs than the nave and are narrower
than the tower. Nevertheless, they indicate a movement
towards the development of towers supported on sturdy
arches which in turn create a true crossing from which
run transepts of conventional proportions.

The chancel arch and that in the west wall of the
tower are misleading in this respect, since they date
from the 15th century and replaced the original Saxon
arches which were almost certainly narrower than these.
The archway into the south transept, which carries the
inscription mentioned above, leads through a wall three
feet thick and is decorated with a large cable moulding on
the angles, not something often found in this period.

There are seven original Saxon windows left in the
church. These are double-splayed, with the light roughly
in the middle of the thick wall and splays running both
inwards and outwards. The other windows date from the
14th, 15th and 16th centuries, except for the big west
window which is modern.

Over the south door is a Saxon *rood* more severely
mutilated than the one at Romsey (see page 204), but
still showing similar features like the hand of God pointing down from a cloud to the head of his crucified son.
In the 15th century frescos were painted to provide a
background for the figures of Christ, the Virgin Mary

and St John and traces of these still reveal a landscape of rolling hills dotted with a church and other buildings, as well as the monogram IHS (originally an abbreviation of the Greek spelling of Jesus, later variously interpreted as Latin *Iesus Hominum Salvator* – Jesus Men's Saviour; *In Hoc Signo* (vinces) – in this sign (thou shalt conquer) and *In Hac (Cruce) Salus* – in this (cross) is salvation) and the initials ABM (*'Ave beata Maria'* – or 'Hail blessed Mary').

All Saints, Brixworth, Northamptonshire

All Saints, Brixworth, is one of the very oldest and most impressive early Saxon churches in the country, having been in constant use since the late 7th century, a matter of barely two or three centuries after the Romans pulled out of Britain. Monks from Peterborough were responsible for its construction only a short time after the area had been converted to Christianity and in general design they followed the form of a basilica, a type of building common in the Roman world.

Their original church was somewhat larger than it is today. The arcades on the north and south sides of the nave probably led originally into a series of small compartments known as *porticuses*, which may possibly have served as side chapels. At the east end they also constructed the *apse*, which has been rebuilt.

One of the church's most distinctive features is the use of roman tiles in the arches and sections of the tower. Excavations in the vicinity have revealed the site of at least one Roman building which may have yielded materials recycled to build All Saints.

The only surviving evidence of Norman building work is the south doorway, which forms the principal entrance today. When the church was first built, however, entry was gained through the western end where the doorway

59

in the tower was later blocked by the round stair turret. Porches were also built on the north and south sides of the tower, as the small doorways there indicate. The building of the stair turret (one of only four of this design in England) at some time in the 9th or 10th centuries significantly altered the appearance of the tower. The turret was built above the earlier Saxon work (marked by the line of the off-set) and gave access into what is now the clock chamber.

At the other end of the church a ring-crypt (one of only four in Europe) was built below the semicircular apse, probably to allow pilgrims to descend to a crypt chapel underneath the apse, where a relic or other treasure would have been housed. Although there is no documentary evidence to prove the theory, there is a reasonable chance that a small piece of bone found bricked up in the south wall of the Lady chapel in 1821, and now kept in the iron cage by the pulpit, may have been such a relic. References in the church records to St Boniface of Crediton, the first English missionary to Europe and the saint who converted the heathens in Germany, suggest that he may have had more than a passing connection with Brixworth. The small piece of bone has been identified as a human larynx bone which has led to the speculation that it may be that of St Boniface himself, a relic beyond compare, brought back to England and housed in an important missionary centre.

There isn't a shred of hard evidence to support this idea, mind you, and no traces of a crypt chapel have been discovered. In fact, in the Middle Ages the apse was replaced by a square-ended chancel; this was only pulled down in the last century so that the apse could be restored.

Of the medieval alterations that do remain, one of the most striking is the great arch that separates the nave from the *presbytery* (the part of the church that lies to the east of it). This was built at the beginning of the 15th century to replace a large triple arch which would have appeared like a screen at the eastern end of the nave. Remains of this arch can still be seen on either side of the existing one, which provides such an impressive view of the arch over the entrance to the apse and of the altar and apse itself. The only significant medieval alterations to the outside of the church were, first, the addition of the Lady chapel in the 13th century and then the spire built in the middle of the century that followed.

Back inside the church, the western arch that leads into the base of the tower stands below a blocked doorway that may originally have led into a gallery. Following the removal of the gallery, the floor levels in the tower were rearranged resulting in the present ringing chamber looking on to the nave through a lovely window, distinctive for its baluster shafts that have been worked by chisel as opposed to being turned on a lathe.

St Augustine, Brookland, Kent

From the outside, Brookland church presents an intriguing picture that would tempt any visitor to stop for a closer look even without knowing what this attractive building offers inside.

Like many churches in Romney Marsh, this is built on an artificial mound to raise it above the dangers of flood water. This has clearly resulted in some settlement since building work began in the middle of the 13th century, as the heavy buttressing outside and the leaning piers inside demonstrate. The church is long and low, with two east gables, and its most distinctive feature is the wooden belfry which stands quite apart from the main building, looking like three candle snuffers stacked on top of each other.

Local theories are rife about the origin of this curious structure. There are suggestions that after two attempts to build a belfry on the church in its conventional location, both of which ended with its being blown down, it seemed wiser to leave it on the ground where it obviously felt more at ease. There are other other accounts of the belfry having been brought to Brookland from Lydd by Cardinal Wolsey, and of its having toppled in astonishment at the marriage of a couple in the parish well advanced in years. Whatever the truth of the belfry's construction, it has aroused some lively speculation and even inspired an eighty-page poem published in 1786 under the catchy title of *The Religion of a Lawyer, a Crazy Tale in four cantos: analytical of the Kentish Story of Brookland Steeple.*

Expert opinion dates the belfry from the middle of the 13th century, making it probably a direct contemporary of the church proper. It seems that that original structure may have been square, and possibly open to the elements, the bells hanging and being rung in a sort of campanile. In the middle of the 16th century a major refurbishment took place in which the original timbers were strengthened, additional ones were added turning the square into its present octagon, the 'spire' was added and, most significantly, the whole structure was clad with wooden shingles. The present cedar shingles were fitted in 1936. Above the belfry is the unusual weather-vane shaped like a mallard in flight and dated 1797 with the initials CS.

The porch on the north side of the church through which one enters St Augustine's was built in the 14th century and has attractive barge boards and *spandrels* (the area between the square frame and the arch within it) decorated with *quatrefoils*.

The interior of the church retains most of its Early English simplicity. In the chancel there are two ascending *sedilia* and a *piscina* on the south side. These have the characteristic pointed arches reflecting the Early English development away from the round arches of the Norman or Romanesque style.

The nave is Early English, too, with seven bays on the south side and six on the north. To add to this asymmetry the piers and arcades lean alarmingly away from the perpendicular, as mentioned earlier. Like Pisa's leaning tower this seems to have been their preferred position for several hundred years without noticeable risk to the overall fabric of the building.

In 1964 repairs to the south wall of the chapel at the east end of the south aisle revealed traces of the wall

painting that now shows the martyrdom of St Thomas
à Becket in Canterbury Cathedral. The chapel also contains the table-top tomb of John Plomer, three times
Mayor of Romney, who died in 1615. As mayor of one
of the Cinque Ports he would have had the honour of
supporting the canopy over James I at his coronation in
1603, a privilege that would have earned him the title of
Baron of the Cinque Ports.

Near the south chapel stands the fine 18th-century
pulpit, preserving two of its original three 'decks'. The
inlaid sounding board that once graced the upper level
from where the sermon was preached is now the top of
the table at the west end of the nave.

The west end of the south aisle, known as the 'Tithe
Pen', formerly housed the set of scales, weights and measures now displayed near the vestry. These include measures for grain and fluids and the brass rod for measuring
bolts of cloth, all of which would have been paid to the
vicar as his tithe by the parishioners.

Across the church, at the west end of the north aisle,
the late medieval vicars of Brookland would have held
their village schools.

Probably the single feature of greatest interest inside
the church, and about which much has been written,
is the circular lead font, one of the very few remaining
lead fonts in the country. This is decorated with the
signs of the Zodiac, below which appear the occupations
for each month, a decorative combination that is again
rare in this country. Twenty months appear in all with
their corresponding signs, the duplication beginning in
March, the month of the spring equinox. The work has
been attributed to Norman or Flemish craftsmen, though
how the font found its way to Brookland is still a subject
for debate. It may have been brought to St Augustine's
church at Canterbury, and subsequently found its way
to the dependent church at Brookland. Alternatively the

font may represent part of the loot seized during a raid on the French coast.

Whatever its origin, the activities picked out throughout the year give a vivid insight to the way in which the medieval working year was structured. In March a hooded figure is seen pruning his vines, seven months later the figure in October is seen treading his grapes to make wine. There is a mower at work in June, a haymaker raking hay in July, a thresher stripped to the waist as he flails his crop with a wooden flail in September, and in the depths of winter a man killing a pig in December to provide food for the cold months ahead, while in February he is seen huddled by his fire to keep warm.

St Mary and St Michael, Cartmel, Cumbria

13 MILES SOUTH-WEST OF KENDAL, OFF B5278

Cartmel lies at the heart of a small peninsula that juts south into Morecambe Bay. Frequently eclipsed by the better-known attractions of the Lake District to the north, it is one of the undiscovered secrets of north-west England.

At its heart stands the priory Church of St Mary and St Michael, a massive cruciform church of near-cathedral proportions that survives as the greatest medieval parish church of the area in addition to being the virtually unique example of a medieval priory church that has survived the Reformation intact.

St Mary and St Michael dates from the end of the 12th century when William Marshall, Baron of Cartmel (later the second Earl of Pembroke) founded an Augustinian priory among the flat fields of the Cartmel peninsula. This he endowed with the manor and lands in the area, together with a number in Ireland. Included among the stipulations he made was the requirement that the priory should maintain an altar and priests for the benefit of the people of the area. This point proved the building's salvation when the Dissolution of the Monasteries that followed the Reformation threatened to sweep it away with so many other religious foundations.

In 1537 Henry VIII's commissioners arrived to strip the monastery and priory of all its possessions. Most of the priory buildings were devastated and allowed to fall into disrepair; just the gatehouse in the centre of the village was left standing. The church did not escape damage. The lead was stripped from the roof and only the parochial right to worship in the priory church saved the building from further destruction. As it was, the south aisle of the choir was designated as the parish church. This became known as the Town Choir and, while worship continued here, the rest of the church and the roof remained exposed to the elements for over eighty years.

In 1618 George Preston of Holker Hall, whose family had acquired much of the former priory land, began restoration work, largely at his own expense. The church was reroofed and Preston enriched it further by the addition of the wonderful oak screen and the canopies placed over the choir-stalls and *misericords*.

The church that he set about saving had grown steadily throughout the Middle Ages. The earliest Norman work can be found in the chancel (though the east window is Perpendicular) and in the wonderful south door. The north transept is Early English. The south chapel, or Town Choir, belongs to the Decorated period, having been enlarged in about 1340.

In the middle of the 15th century the original half dozen *lancet* windows in the east end were removed and in their place the magnificent Perpendicular window was created. Only a small portion of its wonderful glass, made by the York school of glaziers, remains in the three main lights, but this gives some indication of the splendour with which this window greeted worshippers.

The east window had not long been finished when the builders turned their attention to the tower, resetting the upper stage diagonally on the part below, creating a unique structure which cheerfully ignores all architectural rules and is still standing five hundred years later.

Among its many features Cartmel possesses in the Harrington tomb one of the best mid-14th-century tombs in the country.

It is also justly proud of its wealth of carved oak. The choir screen, with its twenty-eight pillars, is of Flemish origin dating from 1620 and is decorated with emblems of Christ's Passion. The choir-stalls and misericords, which were exposed to the elements for eighty years after the removal of the lead, show tremendous craftsmanship and imagination.

The misericords (carved brackets on the little tip-up seats designed to give some support to the clergy condemned to stand for long periods during services) are especially interesting. Since they were largely hidden from view, they allowed the carvers greater liberty than did work widely exposed to the sight of the congregation. Among those at Cartmel are a mermaid with two tails, an elephant and castle, and a doctor represented as an ape holding a flask.

Cartmel's other treasures are a mixed but no less fascinating bag. The church owns a copy of the so-called Vinegar Bible of 1716, which substitutes or misprints the word 'vinegar' for 'vineyard' in the description of the parable in the vineyard at the head of the twentieth chapter of St Luke's gospel. The other great literary treasure is a first edition of Spenser's *Faerie Queene* published in 1596.

Cartmel Priory is also the slightly unexpected owner of one of the very earliest umbrellas, reckoned to be more than 200 years old.

Both St Mary's, Whitby (above), and St Peter and St Paul, Lavenham (below), serve as landmarks above their respective towns.

Both Canute and King Harold came to worship at Holy Trinity, Bosham, in the eleventh century.

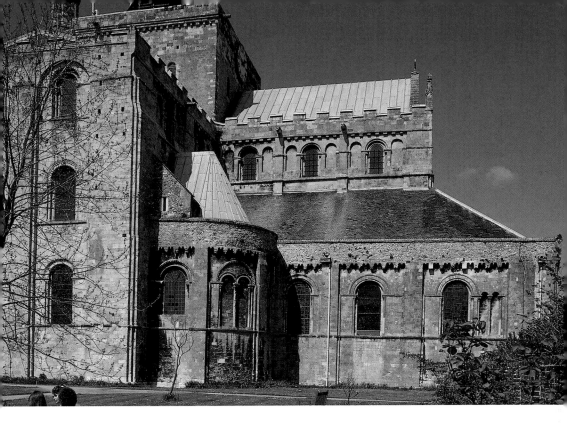

Two of England's most splendid Norman abbeys, Romsey (above) and Tewkesbury (below).

There is a rich feast of decorated work on the south porch of St Andrew's, Heckington.

St Edmund, Castleton, Derbyshire

9 MILES NORTH-EAST OF BUXTON, ON A625

St Edmund's is a Norman church, much restored during the last century. It has a good chancel arch, a Norman font and a 17th-century roof decorated with the portcullis of the Duchy of Lancaster. The tower was built in the Perpendicular style and remains largely unaltered. Early in the 19th century the church was provided with a lending library of well over a thousand volumes collected by the Reverend Frederick Farran who, during his time as Vicar of Castleton, had been in the habit of lending books to villagers. There are several early Bibles in English, dating from the so-called 'Great Bible' of 1539 which Thomas Cromwell, the architect of the Reformation, ordered to be placed in every parish church in England. There is a large collection of 18th-century books, not all of them dealing with religious subjects, and there are several very rare books at Castleton only found elsewhere in the four or five main 'copyright' libraries in the country.

The church's principal interest is in its close relationship with the village. Standing in a marvellous setting with views to the High Peak, it was built below Peveril Castle, the Norman ruin immortalized by Sir Walter Scott in *Peveril of the Peak*. Castleton, as its name implies, grew up around this important fortification and the church, as the most impressive building in the village, was situated on a slight mound.

Around the whole village a large semicircular earthwork was erected during the Middle Ages as further protection and in times of trouble the villagers would retreat into the huge gaping Peak Cavern, the nearest of the area's famous caverns; its smoke-blackened roof is a reminder of those troubled times.

During the 12th century the Custodian of the Castle was responsible for appointing the vicars of Castleton and St Edmund's became known as 'the church of Peak Castle'.

St Edmund's is also the scene of the climax of the annual Garland Day ceremony held in Castleton on Oak Apple Day (29 May, when the escape of the future Charles II from the Battle of Worcester is recalled – he hid in an oak tree). The Garland is a large beehive-shaped construction made of wood and wire to which are attached masses of wild flowers and greenery. At its top sits a smaller but more elegant posy of the best flowers, attached to a foot-long peg. This is known as the Garland Queen.

The Garland is carried by the King, a man dressed in Stuart clothes, and so large is it that he is completely covered from the waist up, so that the horse on which he is mounted has to be led round the village. Accompanying the Garland King is his Lady, riding side-saddle, followed by the band and a procession of dancing girls dressed in white dresses.

The procession makes a tour of the village, pausing for refreshment at each pub, until they eventually make their way to the church; until 1948 it was the bellringers who were responsible for organizing the festivities. The little Queen posy is removed from the Garland, which is then hoisted to the top of the tower straight from the King's shoulders. Once up there, it is placed on the centre pinnacle above the clock, where it stays until the last flower dies, about three weeks later.

Following a display of Maypole dancing by the children on the green, the Queen posy is placed on the village war memorial as the band plays 'The Last Post'.

St Agnes, Cawston, Norfolk

The wealth of the medieval wool trade gave Cawston its beautiful church, dedicated appropriately to St Agnes, whose name sounds similar to the Latin word *agnus* ('a lamb'), which she is shown carrying. Early in the 14th century the church was almost completely rebuilt in the Perpendicular style (the chancel and south transept are Decorated).

The church is impressive from the outside. The tall tower devoid of battlements, pinnacles or even a parapet is heavily buttressed, indicating that a spire may have been intended in the original design. The tower is faced with freestone, so called because it could be sawn or cut in any direction, which was brought from Caen in Normandy. The rest of the church is built of flint bonded with a mix of sand and lime.

Above the south porch is a room that may have served as a vestry, or a 'strong-room' for church treasures, or possibly as a gathering place for the masons. (A room such as this over a church porch is sometimes known as a 'parvis'.)

Still on the south side, just above the chancel, are small sundials that may also have had some connection with medieval masonic custom. Straws stuck into the holes cast shadows to tell the time.

Inside, the church's chief glory is its magnificent hammer-beam roof, one of the finest in the country.

Though no longer richly painted, as it was before the Reformation, this has a beauty in material and design that is hard to match. The oak in the timbers is silver-brown with age. The joints are masked by charming floral bosses. Half-length angels line the *cornice* at the top of the walls, three a side in every bay. The areas behind each hammer-beam (known as *spandrels*) are decorated with intricate tracery, and each beam carries a full-length and fully-feathered angel with wings outstretched – magnificent in their unpainted oak, leaving one speculating how they must have have looked when freshly painted and newly installed.

The *rood screen*, however, does retain its original paintings, the work of Flemish artists who depicted St Matthew (wearing spectacles and carrying a money box with chain) and St Gregory (whose gloves were used as a design for the gloves of the Bishop of Norwich), as well as a number of other saints. They also depicted Master John Schorne (at the far right). He is shown conjuring the devil into a boot and tradition holds that he was well known for the entertainment he provided with his toy 'devil in a boot', which apparently developed into the first jack-in-the-box. Master Schorne was also said to be able to cure gout and Sir John's Well at Marston in Buckinghamshire had connections with him.

In the nave some of the pews date back 250 years, several being decorated with *poppy-heads*. One at the back shows a dog licking its paw, perhaps reminding us that this was where the dogs were mustered during services – for dogs would go to church as well as their masters in times gone by.

The south transept reflects another interesting side to medieval life, the growing power and wealth of guilds. This present-day Lady chapel was originally the chapel of the local weavers' guild, whose funds paid for it and several of whose members are portrayed in the roof bosses. In the south wall is the *piscina*, above which are representations of a dragon and a wild man, or woodwouse, who appeared on the family crest of the De La Poles, the first Earls of Suffolk.

Inside the tower is a medieval bell-frame with eight bells, dating from 1658, which are still chimed by carillon as in the Middle Ages. At the foot of the tower is a little plough gallery recalling another medieval custom, that of the church-ales. These were fund-raising events, pagan in origin and timed to coincide with the agricultural year, which were the forerunners of the modern church fête. Churchwardens provided large quantities of malt which was brewed into ale at the village brew-house and this was then consumed with much joyful and frequently riotous celebration. At Cawston the plough gallery carries the inscription:

'God spede the plow and send us ale corn enow our purpose for to make: At crow of cok of the plowlete of Sygate; Be mery and glade wat good ale yis work mad.'

Many country churches had plough galleries established by the local ploughmen's guild; this at Cawston refers to the guild that met at an inn in the nearby village of Sygate, renamed Southgate in the last century. The inn was originally called the Plough and, when it closed in 1950, the sign was given to the church.

St Katherine, Chislehampton, Oxfordshire

7 MILES SOUTH-EAST OF OXFORD, ON B480

John Betjeman wrote a poem about St Katherine's, Chislehampton; John Piper painted the clock face and wrote in his Shell guide to the county, 'If you are fond of decrying 18th-century art, go and see Chislehampton church, and enjoy it, and prove yourself wrong for once.'

Built in 1762–3, St Katherine's is one of the very few complete and unspoilt Georgian churches left in England. Charles Peers, a prosperous London porcelain merchant, acquired an estate in Chislehampton from the Doyley family, demolished the old church and mansion that stood closer to the River Thame and built in their place this lovely little white church with its distinctive bell turret, and the imposing red-brick house which stands beside it surrounded by its small park dotted with now-stately trees.

The old church, some two hundred yards to the west, had been dedicated to St Mary, but when the new one was consecrated St Katherine (the name of the squire's wife) became its patron and her name can be seen pierced in the weather-vane. The old church provided the roof and three-decker pulpit for the new building, but in all other respects this is a perfectly preserved example of a small 18th-century country church.

Passing through the gates that lead directly on to the road, flanked by stone piers topped with stone balls, the church is approached down a short path with rose beds on either side. Above the double doors stands the pretty wooden bell turret and the clock face that John Piper painted in 1952. Murray's *Handbook to Oxfordshire* observed that the bell turret is 'such as is usually placed on stables' which roused considerable though quite unnecessary criticism, for that is exactly what it is – and this detracts in no way from the pleasing proportions of the simple rectangular building with its plain gabled roof.

Immediately inside the church is the area beneath the gallery supported on a couple of columns. The small vestry is here, along with the font and an empty space that may have been intended for christening parties.

The church retains its distinctive box pews in two blocks on either side of the central alley. Those towards the east are somewhat larger and taller, providing greater privacy than the ones towards the back of the church, the largest and closest to the altar being that of the squire and his family.

The fine three-decker pulpit occupies the space of the second pew from the east on the north side. In an unusual location in the corner of the next pew stands the parish clerk's desk.

The communion table stands inside a small three-sided enclosure of rails running back down the church, parallel with the north and south walls, to join the eastern box pews. Benches once lined the walls inside this enclosure, perhaps providing seating for communicants staying for the service of communion after a previous service.

Modest as it may appear, Chislehampton's large windows, simple architecture and uncluttered furnishings display the best features of an 18th-century country church, which so inspired both Betjeman and Piper.

St John the Baptist, Cirencester, Gloucestershire

16 MILES NORTH-WEST OF SWINDON, ON A419

At the height of the Roman occupation of Britain, Corinium Dubonorum, to give Cirencester its Latin name, grew to become the second most important town in the country. The attendant prosperity that came with this died as the Romans withdrew and it was to be the best part of a thousand years before the wealth of Cirencester returned to anything like its ancient level – and when it did, it came on the back of sheep.

As the generally accepted 'capital of the Cotswolds', Cirencester has the largest and most magnificent of the 'wool' churches in the region, one praised as being the most beautiful Perpendicular church in England.

Seen from a distance the church has a skyline recalling Gloucester Cathedral across the hills along the Roman road heading north-westwards. The nave and aisle roofs are decorated with open tracery ornamental battlements, topped by *crocketed* pinnacles, and the magnificent buttressed tower and three-storeyed south porch overlooking the market place set this apart as a parish church of no ordinary proportions.

Until the dissolution of the abbey at Cirencester in 1539 the church was served by its canons and it was the abbey which was responsible for building the great south porch with its wonderful fan-vaulting in about

77

1500. Its principal function was to provide somewhere for abbey business to be conducted outside the abbey proper. Following the suppression of the abbey, the chamber above the porch became the town hall. By 1836 the porch was in a fairly poor condition and, thanks to the generosity of Earl Bathurst, it was taken down and carefully rebuilt stone by stone, in the course of which the two upper storeys were converted into the present lofty chamber.

The porch was actually finished a few years before work began on rebuilding the Early English nave, but the two blend so well now that it seems highly likely that plans for the nave had already been drawn up or at least taken into consideration when work began on the porch.

Nothing of any substance remains of the previous naves which were taken down to make room for the spectacularly light and airy late Perpendicular structure that distinguishes Cirencester church today. The ceiling stands fifty-seven feet above the floor, suspended it seems by a wall of glass formed by the wide windows of the *clerestory* and the lovely window set over the chancel arch. Building work lasted from 1515 to 1530, marking this as one of the last great Gothic churches to be built in England, completed less than a decade before the Reformation changed the nature and perception of the Church in England for ever.

Succeeding generations added their own paraphernalia in the form of galleries and staircases, but we can thank Gilbert Scott that these were removed when, in the middle of the last century, he set about restoring the church to something like its original appearance.

Among his many changes Scott reinstated the 14th-century font which for two hundred years had been demoted in favour of a small Renaissance font, spending its exile as a flowerpot in the abbey gardens.

The pulpit, on the other hand, was one of the few 'wine-glass' pulpits to survive the Reformation. Standing on a slender stem, it is embellished with finely-carved open stonework which has been recoloured and gilded to look more or less as it must have done when it was first installed.

Up in the east end of the nave wall the church houses its greatest treasure, the Boleyn Cup, in a special safe. The cup was made for Henry VIII's second wife, Anne Boleyn, two years before her execution. Her personal emblem, a falcon holding a sceptre with a rose tree, can be seen surmounting the cover. Anne Boleyn gave the cup to her daughter, destined to become Queen Elizabeth I. She in turn gave it to her physician, Dr Richard Master, who presented it to the parish church after he acquired the lands of the former abbey. Like the pulpit, it is a rare survivor of the Reformation.

The chancel screen dividing the nave from the chancel serves an aesthetic role in spite of presenting certain practical difficulties. Traditionally the chancel was the property of the abbey while the nave belonged to the parishioners. So while the latter rebuilt the nave to match their wealth, the chancel remained unaltered and understandably soon looked out of keeping with the grandeur and opulence that lay to the west of the screen. By retaining this, the contrast between the two parts of the church is less apparent.

That said, the chancel is the oldest part of the church, remaining pretty much as it was in the 15th century. There is 15th-century glass in the east window, including the head of the Devil, shaped rather like a horned bull, and a Roman column supporting the eastern arch on the south side. In contrast, the fine stone *reredos* was designed by Gilbert Scott's son and crowned by his father with a fussy gable that obscured the lower part of the window. Fortunately, this has been removed.

St Catherine's chapel, which stands to the north of the chancel, originally served as its north aisle. The beautiful fan-vaulted roof that adorns it today was donated in 1508 by the penultimate abbot, John Hakeborne. His initials appear in one of the bays along with a bishop's mitre, recording the fact that, although he was not actually a bishop, the abbot carried similar status since Cirencester church was designated a 'mitred abbey'. The other ceiling bosses show the arms of the Prince of Wales and the royal arms of his father, Henry VII.

Through a small Norman archway lies the Lady chapel, entirely rebuilt in the middle of the 15th century when it acquired its handsome carved roof on which the figures of a cat and mouse can be seen eyeing each other from opposite sides of a corn sheaf.

More fine carving is displayed in the early 17th-century Bridges Tomb, commemorating Humphrey Bridges and his wife. The figures are carved with great sensitivity and a naturalness of expression that elevates them far above the frigid piety of so many memorial statues. Around them are gathered their children: three babies who died in infancy, six daughters holding prayer books and, kneeling at either end, their two sons who both died as young men, in advance of their mother.

Cirencester church acquired its fine tower through something of a windfall at the turn of the 15th century. Until that time, from all accounts, the church had no tower. But in 1400 the Earls of Kent and Salisbury attempted an uprising against Henry Bolingbroke, soon to become Henry IV, after they returned to Cirencester having failed to rescue the imprisoned king, Richard II. However, they misjudged the mood of the townspeople and found themselves placed under arrest and locked up in the church. When their supporters began setting fire to houses in the town, the good people of Cirencester responded by chopping off the earls' heads in the marketplace and sending them to King Henry. He in return allowed them to keep the sizeable treasure that the two rebels had planned to use to fund their rebellion, and with it they built the splendid tower. If the lower section looks somewhat plainer than the upper ones, it is probably due to the fact that until the last century houses surrounded the tower, so that only the upper levels could be seen.

All Saints, Claverley, Shropshire

Set on a wooded slope, Claverley is a pretty village of black-and-white timber-framed cottages mingled with buildings of local sandstone and mellowed brick. At its centre stands All Saints Church, built on the site of a Saxon church which in turn probably replaced an even earlier pre-Christian structure, possibly of Roman origin.

All Saints has two fonts, both of them of great age. The oldest is a crudely worked Saxon bowl which helps to place the church for which it was fashioned in the second half of the 7th century. The later one was probably made four hundred years later at around the time of the Norman Conquest. The date of the nave is uncertain, but the absence of any sign of an *apse* in the chancel suggests that it was built before the arrival of the Normans. In any event, Norman changes weren't long in coming for by the end of the 11th century three typically Norman arches were pierced in the north wall, together with the lower portion of the present tower.

By far the most striking feature of the nave and the church as a whole are the wall paintings over the north arcade, which have been dated as early as 1200. Nearly eight hundred years later these are still well preserved and rich in detail, instantly bringing to mind the more familiar images of the Bayeux Tapestry. The subject matter is similar, too, and it was generally assumed

82

that the contests fought between five pairs of knights on horseback represented the Battle of Hastings. Later interpretation introduces an allegorical theme based on a Latin poem widely read in the Middle Ages. In this seven Christian virtues take on seven pagan vices and, if the frieze continued on the western wall, as has been suggested it once did, the number of battling figures could tally with this interpretation.

Later paintings from the 15th century have also been discovered in the *spandrels* of the arches and between the windows of the *clerestory*. Over the chancel arch are visible the remains of a large representation of the Last Judgement, commonly referred to as a Doom.

At about the same time as the building of the chancel arch, around 1500, the west window was inserted along with a new tower arch containing an unusual niche in its massive buttress. The purpose of this is unclear, though suggestions have been made that it may have been designed as a place of penitence or confession.

Among the benefactors of All Saints recorded at the west end of the nave is Mr Richard Dovey who, along with gifts of the clock, communion set and land, made the unusual bequest of eight shillings a year for 'a person for awaking sleepers in the church'. The last holder of this post, one Bobby Ball, used to sport a red waistcoat to carry out his official duties (earning him the nickname Robin Redbreast) and carried a pole with a fox's brush at one end with which he roused any lady who had dropped off during a service. Men who closed their eyes for a moment or two were given a more businesslike poke with the other end of Bobby's pole.

St Andrew, Clifton Campville, Staffordshire

8 MILES EAST OF LICHFIELD, OFF A453

St Andrew's, Clifton Campville, is reckoned by many to be Staffordshire's finest medieval church. Built largely in the Decorated style, it is an enlargement of an older Early English cruciform church, parts of which are still evident in their noticeably rougher masonry.

Among these is the *chantry* chapel, which was formerly the north transept of the earlier church. Traces of painting survive in the arched recess that houses the altar, recalling the pre-Reformation decoration that must have enlivened this lofty, airy church. From early in the 18th century until the end of the last, the chapel served as the household pew of the Pye family, several of whom are remembered in marble monuments around the church, and after their departure from the village it was used as a vestry until being restored to its original use in 1972.

The room above the chapel is a priest's chamber, though this, too, served another purpose in the 18th century when it acted as a temporary schoolroom for some thirty boys and girls from the village.

The north door is the original north door of the old church and in the north wall under a low arch is a tomb believed to be that of Isabella, first wife of Sir Richard Stafford, founder of the later church.

The fine Perpendicular church of St Nonna has stood at the heart of the parish of Altarnun since the Middle
Ages.

The exquisite medieval rood screen (above) runs across the church of St Andrew, Cullompton (below left).
Below right, Wimborne Minster was founded by St Cuthburga in AD 713.

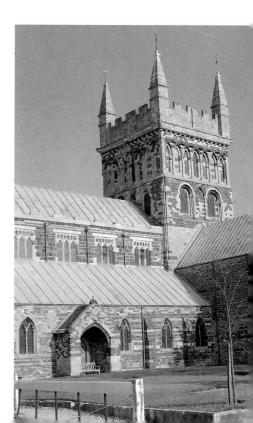

Sir Richard's second wife, named Maud, is possibly the subject of a brass effigy situated in the sanctuary and dating from the middle of the 14th century. Two centuries later Sir John Vernon of Harlaston and his wife Ellen were commemorated in a magnificent Tudor tomb worked in alabaster which stands in the middle of the Lady chapel. This is surrounded by four *parclose screens*, at least two of which are the original Decorated ones; the fourth is a beautifully crafted Carolinian one. Next to the doors of the south screen is the ancient chest of which St Andrew's is justly proud; this was cut from a solid tree trunk.

In the wall of the south aisle is a low arch, thought to contain the tomb of Sir Richard Stafford. The wall painting, uncovered in 1933, shows the Coronation of the Virgin Mary and is a good example of medieval art dating from the 14th century.

St Andrew's is renowned for its magnificent, slender spire, 189 feet in height, with elegant flying buttresses at its base. The tower on which this stands is finely proportioned and, with walls pierced by its three large windows with their delicate tracery and the high arch opening into the nave, it appears to be standing on four huge pillars. Unfortunately the tower is no longer strong enough to withstand the strain imposed by ringing its peal of six bells, so for the last twenty years these have been sounded by a chiming apparatus.

St Andrew, Cullompton, Devon

St Andrew's, Cullompton, is one of Devon's finest and most interesting churches. In the Middle Ages the town was the centre of a prosperous wool trading area, which accounts for the church's splendours.

Built entirely in the Perpendicular style, with the tower and second south aisle (the famous Lane's aisle) added after the other work, St Andrew's is constructed largely of red sandstone.

The visitor enters through the west door in the base of the tower, built in the four years between 1545 and 1549, straddling the reigns of Henry VIII and his son Edward VI. Passing into the western end of the nave you walk under the impressive Jacobean gallery, which is one of the longest in Devon.

The nave piers are worked from Beer stone and are topped by capitals carved with a range of different subjects that include two heads of bearded kings (thought possibly to be Henry VI), the Green man of popular folklore, angels holding scrolls, women with double-peaked head-dresses and finely carved foliage.

St Andrew's has no chancel arch, allowing the magnificent wagon roof an uninterrupted run throughout the entire length of the church. The glorious colours here are a powerful reminder of the gorgeous decoration that there must have been in churches throughout the country before the austerities of the Reformation swept them away or hid them from sight.

In St Andrew's there is a richness of decoration as well as colour. The roof is subdivided into 144 panels, with a carved boss in the centre of each. In addition there are elaborately carved bosses at the apex of the roof, and the wall plates are carved with vine-trail decoration along their entire length.

There is also exquisite vine-trail carving in the wonderful coloured *rood screen* that runs right across the church. This has eleven bays, three for each aisle and five for the nave, with tracery that follows the pattern of the aisle windows. Above the fan tracery of the coving sits the carved cornice, decorated with vine-trail decoration. A series of mortices above this suggests that an additional part of the rood screen, maybe a parapet, sat here; but this has disappeared.

However, it is known that above the central door on top of the rood screen stood the gruesome Golgotha that is now found at the western end of Lane's aisle. This consists of two huge baulks of oak carved with the images of rocks, skulls and bones which formed the base of the medieval *rood*. Into this the cross would have fitted bearing the crucified figure of Christ, while the figures of the Virgin Mary and St John the Evangelist would have stood either side on platforms. When in so many cases the roods and rood screens of the Middle Ages were destroyed completely, St Andrew's is uniquely fortunate in having preserved both its splendid screen and the grim Golgotha.

The roofs of the north and south aisles complement that of the nave and chancel, retaining much of their colour and displaying the same intricacy in their carvings. It is the second south aisle, Lane's aisle which ranks among the church's principal attractions.

John Lane, a wool stapler from Cullompton, undertook

work on what he intended to be his *chantry* chapel in 1526, making it one of the last chapels of this type to be built in England. It is a work of flamboyant optimism. The figures of thirty-two men in Tudor costume, each distinct in design, decorate the lower stages of the piers while from their capitals springs the magnificent fan-vaulting. The *springers* (stones where the arch begins to 'spring') are carved with angels holding a number of emblems, many of which recall John Lane and the trade that made his fortune. His merchant's mark is there, so are a pair of wool shears and a teasel-holder. These general motifs are repeated in the five pendent bosses spaced along the central rib of the roof. Each of these is decorated with four angels bearing shields, several of which carry similar emblems. Among the religious motifs are the five wounds of Christ on the easternmost boss (the heart is on the centre of the boss below); Judas's hand with a bag of silver; a hand bearing the nails of the Crucifixion; and Christ's head and a cloth.

Outside the church, the western side of the tower once carried the arms of Edward VI and Bishop Veysey of Exeter beside the west window, but these have eroded badly. The remains of a Crucifixion can still be seen above the window, again badly weathered, but with enough remaining to indicate the degree of detail it originally contained.

On the south side the tower has a two-light window flanked by panels bearing the arms of Manning and Whiting. Still on the south side of the church, the exterior decoration of Lane's aisle has suffered from erosion that has obscured many of its fine details. John Lane's mark is much in evidence. There are also finely worked carvings of medieval ships, a memorial inscription to John Lane and his wife, a frieze showing details from the life of Christ and beautifully worked tracery.

Even the guttering at Cullompton is worth attention; look out for the lead downpipes dated 1724.

St Luke and All Saints, Darrington, West Yorkshire

Built of Tadcaster limestone, Darrington church stands in its good-sized churchyard as one of the most pleasing churches in the former West Riding. Inside the lovely Early English south doorway with its deeply moulded arch lies a medieval interior of great interest.

There is an unusual *rood* stair turret added in the 15th century, from which runs a unique little arcaded gallery carried over the north aisle. Quite why it was built remains unsolved. Since it ends in a main pillar of the chancel arch, that rather rules out the idea that it might have been used to gain access to the *rood loft*. Perhaps it was used to observe relics housed in the church, while providing a view of the church interior at the same time.

Some of the bench ends retain their original Perpendicular tracery, and the *misericords* in the chancel stalls are well worth seeing.

Darrington church also possesses a fascinating stone crucifix from the late 12th century. This contains several unusual features. The cross on which the sculptor has depicted Christ has two horizontal beams, the lower slightly wider than the upper. The manner of the crucifixion itself differs from the more familiar represesentation, for instead of being shown with crossed feet, fastened by a single nail, Christ's feet are shown here nailed

89

independently, so that His body is attached to the cross by four nails instead of the usual three. The ball-flower decoration that also appears on the crucifix helps to pin-point its date to some time no earlier than the late 12th century, and the shape of the cross (which bears similarities to a Greek cross) suggests that the design may have originated as a result of the crusades that were undertaken at that time, notably by Richard I.

Anyone who has left the A1 and stopped at Darrington for a breather might care to reflect on the fate of another traveller 300 years ago whose memorial stone stands in the north wall. In July 1671 a Scotsman by the name of Alexander Blair was riding south to London when he fell from his horse in a fit of apoplexy and died as he passed through the village!

St Mary, Deerhurst, Gloucestershire

Over a thousand years ago the small village of Deerhurst sitting in the willowy meadows beside the river was the spiritual centre of Hwicce, a Saxon kingdom of the lower Severn vale. There was a monastery here, one that was well established by the time that Bede was writing in the early 8th century. Many royal heads of Hwicce were buried at Deerhurst, and it was at Deerhurst that Edmund Ironside and Canute met to redefine the boundaries of Saxon and Danish England in the year 1016. By that stage, however, Deerhurst's prominence was on the wane, the ancient monastery being overshadowed by the later foundations in the area, notably at Gloucester and Evesham; by the turn of the 12th century even the neighbouring monastery at Tewkesbury had overtaken Deerhurst in regional importance.

Today the church with its tall thin tower ranks as one of the most valuable and significant Saxon buildings in the country, preserving many interesting Saxon remains and reflecting at least three separate stages of Saxon development from the 7th century or even earlier. There are blocked doors and windows that provide clues to the changing structure and design, and details of sculpture and other decoration that show a range of artistic influences and several designs far advanced for their period.

The font at Deerhurst, to take one example, is reckoned the be the finest Saxon font in existence. It must also be one of the luckiest, having been found in a farm-house nearby where it was doubling as a very serviceable washtub. Dating from the early 9th century, the font is decorated with the Celtic trumpet spiral and bordered with the vine scroll, a motif that has associations with Northumbria.

High in the west wall the church has another architectural treasure in the double triangular-headed east window which is the most elaborate opening in any Saxon church surviving from the 10th century.

The sanctuary arch, built during the third Saxon phase, is also distinctive both for its size and decoration. The carved animal heads on either side of the square hood (known as *label-stops*) are unique to the church and are reminiscent of the figureheads of Scandinavian warships. The third period builders also constructed an *apse* at Deerhurst. This was their greatest achievement and in spite of the fact that only one bay survives and the apse served for part of its history as a cider house, what does remain gives some idea of the quality of its original decoration. The most celebrated feature of this is the carving of an angel which has been likened to those illustrated in the Book of Kells.

Not all Deerhurst's attractions are Saxon, though. The west window of the south aisle contains the oldest glass in the church which comes from the 14th and 15th centuries. Two panels show St Catherine with her wheel and St Alphege, who served as a monk at Deerhust before become Archbishop of Canterbury in which capacity he was martyred by the Danes in 1012. At the west end of the north aisle is a window in memory of Hugh Edwin Strickland of Apperley Court. Below the window is a turkey cock, the crest of the Apperley branch of the Stricklands, one of whom reputedly sailed to North America with the Cabot expedition and returned bringing turkeys with him.

Among the many unusual features of St Mary's must be included the arrangement of pews in the choir, which retains the pattern popular during the Puritan period in both style and substance, the woodwork being richly Jacobean.

If these weren't reason enough for making the short diversion to Deerhurst from the Gloucester-Tewkesbury road, the village has a further claim to distinction in being one of only two in the country possessing *two* Saxon churches. For in 1885 a timber-framed house close to the church was found to contain a small, complete church dating from the late Saxon period. A stone found in an orchard near the house in 1675, and now preserved in the Ashmolean Museum in Oxford, records that the chapel was dedicated to the Holy Trinity and consecrated in 1056 by Odda, a cousin of Edward the Confessor, in memory of his brother. An exact replica of the Odda stone is mounted in the chapel today and is considerably more legible and decipherable than the rather battered guide pasted on a board and propped against one of the windows. Visit on a quiet day and give your imagination free rein – 'Deerhurst' means the 'forest of wild animals'.

St Peter and St Paul, Dorchester-on-Thames, Oxfordshire

8 MILES SOUTH-EAST OF OXFORD, OFF A423

The opening of the bypass across the fields on the other side of the River Thames restored tranquillity and dignity to Dorchester, befitting one of the oldest 'cities' in England.

Free from the almost constant stream of traffic that used to drive through along the busy Oxford–Maidenhead road, Dorchester is a village of great charm today, with only its abbey and the archaeological remains of early settlements in nearby meadows to remind the visitor that it was an important centre in southern England from the Bronze Age until the Norman Conquest.

The Romans established their town between the present village and the River Thames and in the year 634 another Italian visitor, St Birinius, arrived to establish the Christian faith in the Thames Valley and beyond. Birinius's first significant act was to baptize Cynegils, King of the West Saxons, a sacrament that he performed in the waters of the River Thames that flows close to the present abbey. With the king converted, Birinius founded a bishopric whose territory reached to the borders of Northumbria, as Bede recorded in some detail.

Dorchester remained a 'city' until the Norman Conquest when the see was moved to Lincoln and Remigius, the last Bishop of Dorchester, became the first bishop in the new diocese. The cathedral then passed to the Augustinian order until Henry VIII dissolved the monasteries and the first vicar was appointed.

Entering into the south-west aisle, you arrive in the mid-14th century church that served the parishioners of Dorchester. Ahead is the altar, raised on a platform of four steps above a small crypt, and behind it are the remains of the 14th-century wall paintings that formed the original *reredos*.

Dorchester has several features of particular interest and importance, two of them in this part of the church. One is the lead font dating from the first quarter of the 12th century. There are only a few left in the country and Dorchester is fortunate to have one of the best of these. The other remarkable feature is the so-called 'monks' corbel' on the pier near the font. This beautiful mid-14th-century carving warns against the sins of sloth and indolence by showing a group of snoozing monks, snugly wrapped in their habits and obviously quite lost to the divine office to which they should have been paying attention.

Passing inwards, you step into the nave of the great Norman church that stood on the site of the Saxon cathedral. The transitional Norman chancel arch still shows the place of the original crossing where access would have been gained to the north and south transepts through low rounded Norman arches which were replaced early in the 17th century by the larger arches we see today. The northern part of the north transept was demolished, along with the cloisters that adjoined it, and a new north wall was built early in the 17th century. In 1963 the doorway into the cloister garden was opened and a new oak door fitted.

Still on the north side of the church, the north aisle (the chapel of St Birinius, whose shrine was found in 1870 in the doorway later opened into the garden in 1963) dates from the late 13th century. The saint is seen in the east window receiving his missionary orders from the Pope and the other windows display the fine geometric tracery that typifies stone carving of the period; you can get a good impression of this by looking at the windows from the outside. Next to the outside door in the north aisle is an opening with a blocked-up flue which may have been used to bake the wafers used for mass, or possibly to warm the priest's hands on chilly winter mornings.

The screens that divide the chancel from the north and south aisles are reproductions of those installed in the 14th century and include a few pieces of the originals. The double *piscina* at the north-western corner of the sanctuary shows where the high altar of the Norman church would have stood; the magnificent sanctuary that now extends eastwards beyond it was built in the mid-14th century.

Here Dorchester possesses some of its greatest treasures. The east window which immediately catches one's attention has wonderful flowing tracery in its lower parts and ball-flower ornament up at the top of the arch. A good deal of the glass comes from the 14th century, too. You can see St Birinius preaching to the recently converted King Cynegils in one of the panels, St Michael appears in another, killing a dragon, and poor St Lawrence is there, too, with the gruesome gridiron on which he was martyred. The groups of figures carved on the tracery midway up the east window show scenes from Christ's Passion and Resurrection.

The south window in the sanctuary shows the heraldic shields of local families who donated the money for the construction of the sanctuary. Below it are the double *piscina* and *sedilia* whose exquisitely worked canopies are one of the abbey's greatest treasures. The oldest glass in the abbey, dating from the 12th century, is here too in the openings behind the seats, showing scenes from St Birinius's life.

Perhaps the single greatest work at Dorchester stands on the north side of the sanctuary. This is the celebrated Jesse window, with its tree branches of stone growing from the recumbent figure of Jesse lying on the sill and supporting Old Testament prophets and kings. Puritan troops destroyed the figures of Christ and the Virgin and Child at the top, but the other figures remain to be admired.

In the course of his restoration work at Dorchester, which included completely reroofing the church, Sir Gilbert Scott removed from the chancel the three tombs that now stand below the altar steps in the Lady chapel (the eastern portion of the south aisle). The effigy on the northern side is that of a 14th-century Governor of nearby Wallingford Castle, Sir John Seagrave. Against the south wall is the effigy of Judge Stonor, a 14th-century Lord Chief Justice from the reign of Edward III, who lived at Stonor House in the hills near Henley-on-Thames. Between them lies the finest of the three: the magnificent and much admired effigy of Sir John Holcomb, who died during the Second Crusade of 1147–8.

St Peter and St Paul, Easton Maudit, Northamptonshire

6 MILES SOUTH OF WELLINGBOROUGH, OFF A509

Easton Maudit is one of the lesser-known, but nonetheless delightful, Decorated churches of Northamptonshire, and like so many others it is surmounted by a graceful spire, which in this case is supported by elegant pierced flying buttresses.

Most of the present church was constructed in the first half of the 14th century, leaving only the upper part of the tower and the spire to be added early in the following century. Though restored in the 19th century, the church retains many of its original features. The south doorway still has its venerable oak door with its excellent ironwork. In the chancel the *piscina* and triple *sedilia* can still be seen (thanks to a considerable amount of restoration). More amazing perhaps is the survival of the 18th-century font which Pevsner describes as a 'beautiful gadrooned bowl of stone on a square base'. ('Gadrooned' means it has an ornamental edge, like inverted fluting.)

Besides the charm of the building itself, the church has interesting literary connections with no lesser figures than Dr Johnson, Oliver Goldsmith and David Garrick. These came about through the incumbency of Easton Maudit's most famous vicar, Thomas Percy, who lived in the parish from 1753 until 1780.

98

Percy was a scholar and man of letters and during his time at Easton Maudit he amassed, edited and published his famous collection of ballads under the title *Reliques of Ancient English Poetry* (it was published in 1765). In the preface Percy expressed his great thanks to Dr Johnson whom he described as standing 'first in the world for northern literature'.

The year before Johnson had paid an extended visit to Easton Maudit in the company of 'Miss Williams', a regular companion in the years following Mrs Johnson's death. Percy was in the thick of his work and Johnson stayed on to help him with it.

In the preface the author also acknowledges the debt he owed to David Garrick, of whom he wrote, 'in Mr Garrick's collection of old plays are many scarce pieces of ancient poetry, with the free use of which he indulged the editor in the politest manner'.

Goldsmith was an even closer friend. It was Percy who first introduced him to Johnson and who wrote a life of Goldsmith which was prefixed to his miscellaneous works published in 1801.

In spite of these apparent distractions, there is no evidence that Thomas Percy neglected his pastoral duties in Easton Maudit. Unlike so many of his fellow clergy at that time, he seems to have applied himself diligently to his work in the parish. As might be expected, he took particular care of the church registers and had them bound in a single volume. And his old friend Johnson obviously regarded him as a sound example to young men entering the church for he wrote to a young clergyman in 1780 and quoted Percy's maxim 'that it might be discerned whether or no there was a Clergyman resident in a parish, by the civil or savage manners of the people'.

St Mary the Virgin, Eaton Bray, Bedfordshire

Until the discovery of the stone-beds at nearby Tottern-hoe in the 11th century, building stone was scarce in this area on the border of Buckinghamshire and Bedfordshire. As a result the original church at Eaton Bray was probably built of wattle and daub, with a thatched roof.

The present church dates from the beginning of the 13th century, although from the outside it appears to be entirely 15th century.

The first sight of the wonders that Eaton Bray promises inside comes from the south door. This is fitted with late 13th-century ironwork attributed to the celebrated Bedfordshire ironworker, Thomas de Leighton. He was one of the master smiths of the period who was also probably responsible for the doors at the nearby churches of All Saints, Leighton Buzzard and All Saints, Turvey. Thomas de Leighton's reputation spread far beyond Bedfordshire, however. In 1291, Henry de Lewes, the royal smith to Edward I, died and it was to Thomas de Leighton that the king turned to make the grille of Queen Eleanor's tomb in Westminster Abbey.

The south door at Eaton Bray is fitted with three hinges from which flow ornamental scrollwork of astonishing intricacy and delicacy, together with a scrolled ornamentation at the top of the door, which occupies the area where the *tympanum* of an earlier Norman doorway would have been set below the top of the arch.

Carved in the wall on the right-hand side of the door you can still see the remains of a *mass dial* where the hours of services would have been scratched in the form of a crude sundial.

To the left of the door stands the font, a fine Early English example, with four detached columns decorated with exquisite foliage standing at the corners. This deserves more than a casual glance, for here and in the nave Eaton Bray possesses some of the most perfect Early English carving to be seen anywhere. The chalk from Totternhoe may not weather well externally, but inside the ease with which it can be carved, especially when freshly quarried, has resulted in carved capitals, richly moulded arches and clustered piers of great beauty.

The capitals are carved in the *stiff-leaf* style that typifies the purity of Early English work. The south arcade was built around 1220 and the carving here is tightly curled and correspondingly plainer than that in the north arcade, which was built some twenty years later with a looser, more exuberant foliage, confidently undercut.

The carvings on the *corbels* (painted in recent years) are thought to represent people living in the village at the time of the church's restoration in the fifteenth century. These support the roof, which was raised at that time; the line of the 13th-century roof is still visible above the arches in the nave.

The major changes to the design that took place during this period resulted directly from changes in ownership of the manor brought about by the Battle of Bosworth in 1485. Until that time the manor of Eaton, as it was then known, was in the hands of the Cantelou family; the Norman baron, William de Cantelou, having begun the building work on the church. His descendant John de la Zouche fought alongside Richard III at the Battle of Bosworth and lost his lands when Richard lost the battle. However, one Reginald Bray was also fighting on Bosworth Field that day, and apparently it was he who removed the fallen crown from the dead king and handed it to his victor, Henry Bolingbroke, later crowned Henry VII.

Five years later, Sir Reginald Bray, as he had now become, was granted the manor of Eaton (which henceforth became known as Eaton Bray). He was closely involved with the design of St George's Chapel, Windsor, where his head can be still be seen carved in stone on the exterior. So it was only natural that he should turn his attention to the small church in his newly acquired estate, beginning work first on the tower. (This has changed shape considerably since his day and was completely restored during the early part of this century.)

It is likely that Sir Reginald Bray designed the stonework around the east window in the Lady chapel. If this is indeed the case, it is a beautiful memorial to his creative powers. Still in the Lady chapel, one of the stones in the south wall shows the mark in the shape of an 'R' on its side. This represents an instrument known as a hemp brake or 'bray' and, as a pun on his name, was used by Sir Reginald Bray as a building mark.

Two other two tools from the Middle Ages hang on the rear wall of the nave. These are the huge iron and oak thatching hooks that were used to drag burning thatch and timbers from flaming buildings in the days before fire brigades were on hand to deal with calamities like these more efficiently.

The Priory Church of St Mary, St Katharine and All Saints, Edington, Wiltshire

4 MILES EAST OF WESTBURY, ON B3098

Standing below the steep northern escarpment of Salisbury Plain, Edington has one of the outstanding early Perpendicular churches in the country, illustrating the transitional period between the earlier flowing style of the Decorated period and the stiffer lines that came with the shift to the Perpendicular. After Salisbury Cathedral it is the most perfectly proportioned church in Wiltshire and stands as the best surviving example of a collegiate church in southern England.

Cruciform in shape, the church has a central tower, a chancel of three bays that served as the choir for the resident monks and a nave which provided a parish church. The monastery has long since disappeared, with only the great stone walls and fishponds to remind us of its presence. But the church recalls the former glories the monastery once enjoyed and drew from no lesser authority than Pevsner the acclamation 'wonderful'.

It was William of Edington, a native of the parish and later Bishop of Winchester, who founded a college of priests here in 1352. This was later transformed into a monastery for Augustinian canons at the behest of the Black Prince. The foundation stone

103

was laid in 1352 and the church was consecrated nine years later by the Bishop of Salisbury, whose consecration crosses both inside and outside can still be seen.

From the outside the contrast between the part of the church reserved for the parishioners and that of the monastery is immediately noticeable in the windows, those in the aisles and *clerestory* being relatively small and simple, while the windows of the transepts and chancel are considerably more elaborate. This distinction is repeated inside the church, where the choir contains rich mouldings in contrast to the plainer masonry and comparative lack of carving in the part of the church used by the parishioners.

The three-storeyed south porch at Edington is slightly later than the rest of the church. Above the fine stone vault are two chambers, the lower of which is still used as a store-room. A number of monuments and other items were brought to Edington after the neighbouring parish and church of Imber were lost to military use; the Army has retained them since taking them over as a training ground during the Second World War. Among these were the two early 14th-century stone effigies of armoured knights lying in the western end of the south aisle, both of whom represent members of the Rous family, lords of the manor of Imber. The handsome canopied tomb at the eastern end of the south aisle, though unmarked, is probably that of Sir Ralph Cheney who lived nearby and died in 1401.

At the east end of the north aisle stands the 16th- or 17th-century altar of St Giles that was brought from Imber church. At the western end of that aisle is the baptistery created at the end of the 19th century, incorporating a medieval stem with the Victorian marble font and 17th-century font cover.

The windows on this side of the church are shorter than those on the south side, due to the monastery buildings that butted against the north wall.

The panelled plaster ceiling of the nave is 17th century, as are the fine pulpit and canopy. The nave altar that stands on the site of the altar that originally served the parishioners was placed there in 1891, marking the spot where the original altar stood at the time of the monastery.

At the same period of the church's history the north transept served as a Lady chapel; but traces of a painted lily (symbolizing the Virgin Mary) were found inside. The glass in the east and west windows, showing respectively the Crucifixion and angels with musical instruments, is contemporary with the church, two examples of the considerable amount of ancient glass that is still preserved at Edington.

Across the church, the south transept serves as the chapel of St George. The parish war memorials are here and so is the altar tomb of a recumbent figure thought to be a monk, though his identity remains obscure. His feet rest on a barrel (or 'tun') which has been taken to mean that his surname ended with 'ton'. On the cornice of the canopy over the tomb an angel holds a shield bearing an image of a sprig growing out of a barrel, which has been interpreted as a rebus (the teasing representation of a name by pictures suggesting its syllables). This is repeated several times on other parts of the tomb. Beckington or Baynton are both names associated with the parish that provide possible identities. However, the initials TB or IB that are shown on the barrel have led to the suggestion that perhaps the man commemorated was Thomas Bulkington, the benefactor of a house for whom a *chantry* was established. The position was further confused when doubt was cast on whether the figure on the tomb really was a monk. This came about a little over twenty years ago when restoration work revealed that the robe he wears was originally blue, which leaves the man's true identity even more uncertain.

In about 1500 the double screen or *pulpitum* that divides the nave from the chancel was erected, completely blanking off the two parts of the church at that time and only admitting a view of the high altar through the upper parts of the central doors.

Through the screen the chancel is large and well decorated, 'an exquisite composition, not overdecorated yet of the finest craftsmanship in the manifold but subdued enrichments,' as Pevsner describes it. The niches flanking the east window and between the windows on either side are empty now, except for two that contain their mutilated statues. The *sedilia* suffered as well when the Lewis monument was originally placed there. The doorway nearby beneath an ogee-shaped canopy with *crocketed* pinnacles at the side may once have led into a watching chamber against the outside of the church wall, which looks as if it was removed before the Reformation.

The Lewis monument, superbly worked from alabaster and marble, dates from shortly after the death of Sir Edward Lewis in 1630. He lies beside his wife, Lady Anne Beauchamp, who survived him by thirty-four years and the date of whose death was added to the tomb with paint that has subsequently disappeared. Above them hovers a naked cherub bearing a crown of glory while their five children kneel in prayer in front of the tomb. The three youngest may appear to be girls, but at that time boys were dressed as girls until they were seven years old, and only the youngest of the Lewis children, the one with the slightly more elaborate cap, is in fact a girl. The two figures in front of her are actually the young Lewis sons, the younger of whom has leading reins attached to the shoulders of his dress, suggesting that he was probably still under two years old.

St John the Evangelist, Elkstone, Gloucestershire

For over a dozen miles the A417 runs north-west in an almost straight line from Cirencester, 'the capital of the Cotswolds', as it follows the old Roman road of Ermine Street in the direction of Gloucester and the Severn Vale. Elkstone, lying high in the Cotswold Plateau, is one of a number of small villages that have grown up on the sites of ancient settlements dotted on either side of this important thoroughfare. Winstone, Syde, the Duntisbournes and Daglingworth, all of which lie within only a few miles of Elkstone, possess churches of great age and provide the focus for a charming tour that avoids the heavy traffic now thundering down the road the legions once trod. At Elkstone, however, the visitor finds one of Gloucestershire's most celebrated Norman churches.

Elkstone takes its name from the Saxon meaning 'the stone (or stone building) of Ealac' and the village is recorded in the Domesday Book. Although no individual stone can be directly linked with this origin, there is one now standing against the wall in the vestry which scholars believe may date from the 10th century and which carries an interesting non-Christian design. This was moved inside from the churchyard several years ago and there is a faint possibility that this is the stone that gave the village its name.

The exterior decoration at Elkstone is worth careful study. The *tympanum* above the south door is regarded as being one of the very best in the country. As the main entrance to the church, this marked a metaphorical doorway to Christian life and was often the most intricately decorated feature of the exterior of a small church (Kilpeck, across the Herefordshire border, is the outstanding example in this respect.)

At Elkstone the semicircular panel above the south door shows Christ seated centrally on a throne holding the Book of Judgement in his left hand and giving the Blessing with his right. Surrounding him are the symbols of the four evangelists: the winged man of St Matthew, the ox of St Luke, the lion of St Mark and the eagle of St John. The Agnus Dei, or Lamb of God, representing Christ's sacrifice, is on the left and above the seated figure is the hand of God the Father.

The beaked-head frieze that surrounds the *tympanum* is a very well-preserved example of this common Romanesque ornamention.

Another Norman feature well represented at Elkstone (and even better at Kilpeck) is the carving on the *corbel-table*, which was originally built to carry the eaves of the roof, so throwing rainwater clear of the walls and foundations. The animals, birds and signs of the Zodiac that decorate the individual corbels at Eklstone are both well carved and remain for the most part in very good condition.

On the north side there is a fragment of *corbel-table* butting on to a shallow buttress which is all that remains of the original tower that collapsed and was removed in the 13th century. The Perpendicular tower which greets the visitor so impressively today was built by local masons some two centuries after the Norman tower was demolished. In its fine proportions this shows the influence of Gloucester Cathedral. Although the four gargoyles at each corner of the parapet have suffered a little from decay, two of the figures on the set-offs are still well defined; one is playing a stringed instrument known as a citole, the other a wind instrument called a shawm, which was rather like an oboe.

Inside the church your eye is drawn to the lovely east window which forms the focal point of Elkstone's delightful chancel. The stained glass is comparatively modern, replacing hideous Victorian glass, but it complements the zigzag chevron moulding from eight centuries before. The moulded vaulting-ribs of the chancel meet in a boss formed by grotesque faces strapped together, a most unusual feature. The brackets supporting the base of these vaulting ribs were originally decorated with the emblems of the evangelists, but only St Mark's remains intact, along with a fragment of St Luke's.

Above the chancel is a dovecot (*columbarium*), which was created when the roof of the chancel was raised to that of the nave. This is also a very unusual feature to find in a parish church.

Saxon Church, Escomb, County Durham

Very little is known about the history of the small Saxon church that lies at the bottom of a steep road in this former pit-village. There is not even any record of its dedication. But while it remained obscure and overlooked down the centuries, it survives today as one of the most complete small Saxon churches in England.

Archaeological and architectural evidence suggests that the church was built towards the end of the 7th century, making it contemporary with those at Jarrow and Monkwearmouth. The porch was added in the 12th century and the five larger windows in the 13th and 19th centuries, but apart from these alterations the church stands pretty much as it has done for 1,300 years.

For all but its upper courses the church is built of good-sized squared stones, many of them marked with a criss-cross pattern known as 'diamond broaching'. This was a feature of Roman stonework prepared for plastering and leads to the suggestion that much of the material for Escomb church might have been brought from the old Roman fort of Vinovium, or Binchester as it's now known, which is a couple of miles away across the river. The effort involved in transporting this quantity of building stone shouldn't be underestimated, however, and it suggests that Escomb was a site of more than ordinary

110

religious significance to the people who constructed the church here.

There are several other Roman features incorporated into the building, both inside and out. Above the door on the outside of the north wall of the nave is a stone with a rosette carved on it which may have come from a Roman altar used in the building work. In the same wall is another stone with a small ledge which gives some protection to the inscription beneath of the Roman numeral VI (shown upside down). At one time it was also possible to read the word 'LEG' but this has now faded. This has led to the speculation that the inscription may have referred to the Roman 6th Legion which replaced the 9th Legion at York in about AD 122.

Inside the church the small Saxon window closest to the sanctuary in the north wall has a supporting stone with another Latin inscription on its side: ' *Bono rei publicae nato* ', meaning 'to the man born for the good of the state', a phrase used to honour Roman emperors or notable officers of the Empire and one which may have been inscribed on the base of a statue or of an ornate mile post.

The slim round-headed chancel arch seems very well constructed in comparison with those of other churches of the Saxon period; arches were not their builders' strong point, and it's likely that this, too, may originally have been a Roman arch reassembled in Escomb church. The arrangement of the stonework in the jambs of the arch is typically Saxon none the less, with one stone laid upright and the next flat and so on. This has become known as 'Escomb style – long and short'.

Though younger than the fabric of the church, the font is thought to date from the 10th or 11th century, though it may be earlier since its depth allowed for the total immersion of babies during their baptism. Near the font a patch of the original cobble-stone floor has been preserved.

There is uncertainty, too, about the age of the stone cross standing behind the altar. It may have been designed as a standing cross or grave cover, possibly dating from the 9th century. On the other hand it is possible that it may be considerably older, possibly even part of the original 'preaching cross' that stood on the site before the church was built. Fragments of two other Saxon crosses can be seen in the porch.

From the outside you'll see that the porch has two sundials. The upper one is thought to date from early in the 17th century, but the one to its right (in the centre of the south wall of the nave) is reckoned to be the one first added to the church, making it the oldest sundial still in its original place in the country. Above the dial is a crown surmounting a curved serpent, which looks similar to other representations of the pagan creator-god worshipped by the Angles who came to Northumbria and Yorkshire before the arrival of Christianity. If this connection is valid, it provides a graphic example of the early Church incorporating established symbolism to represent the life-giving properties of the Christian Lord.

A couple of gravestones near the porch carry engravings open to different interpretations in different ages. The skull and crossed bones that we associate with pirate flags, and regard as a symbol of death and destruction, was regarded with favour by the faithful of the medieval church who saw them as the means by which resurrection could be achieved on Judgment Day. As such they were symbols of hope and of eternal life – much as this little Saxon church, apparently forgotten during centuries of change, now stands as a solid reminder of some of the earliest stirrings of the Christian faith in England thirteen centuries ago.

St Mary the Virgin, Felmersham, Bedfordshire

Standing majestically among trees above the River Great Ouse, that sweeps round the hill on which the village of Felmersham stands and passes under the five arches of the stone bridge built in 1818, the parish church of St Mary is one of the most impressive parish churches in the country. In spite of later changes to the nave and tower, it is also one of the very best Early English churches in Bedfordshire.

From the outside the beautifully arcaded western front is the most striking feature. This is in three stages. At the bottom stands the deeply moulded central doorway with slender shafts. On either side are blank arches with blank tracery. Above these is a lovely wall arcade consisting of seven bays with arches decorated in the familiar dog-tooth design and springing from decorated capitals that stand on four slender round shafts detached from the wall. The uppermost stage has a wide segmental arch which now contains three Perpendicular windows from the 14th century, probably replacing three earlier *lancet* windows. On either side are narrower pointed arches, each enclosing a tall lancet window. In the 15th century the steep-sided gable end was replaced by the low-pitched parapet topped by the original 13th-century cross.

113

Before going inside, take a look at the tower which is now surmounted by a battlemented parapet and characteristic tower in the south-east corner, built in the late Middle Ages in the Perpendicular style. This replaced the *broach* spire that had originally adorned the tower. However, in conjunction with the raising of the nave walls to create a flat-pitched roof and the creation of the *clerestory*, this serves only to enhance the cruciform shape based on the general plan of chancel, nave and shallow transepts.

The interior of the church has a nobility and grandeur seldom found in country churches. The nave is lined with alternating round and octagonal pillars. The *corbels* above the arches show that they were originally intended to support a far heavier roof when it was pitched like that of the chancel. The crossing is stately and, for once, not overshadowed by the central tower.

Dividing the chancel from the nave is the fine painted three-bayed *rood screen* which sadly lost its *roof loft* during restoration work in the middle of the last century. The long chancel received more attention than other parts of the church in the Victorian restorations. The east window was reformed in the Decorated style, replacing the Early English triple lancet one. Windows were also added east and west of the chancel door, mirroring the style of those already in existence.

The sanctuary has a double *piscina*, an aumbry with doors with heavy metal supports. The oak chairs and altar table are Jacobean. There was a rather unsatisfactory *reredos* in the sanctuary but this was removed in 1950.

In 1956 three new bells were added to the celebrated peal of five, though according to tradition the original five bells were once six. This is partly borne out by the 500-year-old stone and thatch village inn called the Six Ringers. Its sign shows six ringers sharing five bells, the missing one having reputedly been stolen from St Mary's by monks from the neighbouring village Odell, who then lost it when their boat capsized in the river on their way home.

Whatever the monks from Odell may have got up to, their brothers from the monastic settlement at Felmersham are traditionally credited with building the tithe barn that faces the south side of the church. Some accounts date this earlier than the church itself, though no record of it exists before the middle of the 15th century.

St Cuthbert, Fishlake, South Yorkshire

According to tradition, this small village beside the River Don was the most southerly of the resting-places to which the body of St Cuthbert was taken during the seven years in the 10th century, when his band of faithful monks carried him around the north of England, dodging Danish invaders.

Cuthbert was born in northern England during the first half of the 7th century. When he was thirty he was made Prior of Lindisfarne (the present-day Holy Island). At the age of forty he retired as a hermit to one of the inner Farne islands. And in the year 685 he became Bishop of Lindisfarne, an office he held for only two years, dying on 20 March 687.

Undistinguished and withdrawn as his life might appear to have been, St Cuthbert embodied the spirit of the fledgeling religion he espoused. For his simple humility and love of the world he became revered among his followers, so that when Lindisfarne was sacked by Danish invaders, the monks fled with the saint's body and wandered with it throughout the North until 999, when the body of Cuthbert was finally laid to rest in Durham Cathedral.

Today his figure stands in a canopied niche above the west window in the church's imposing tower. In his hand

116

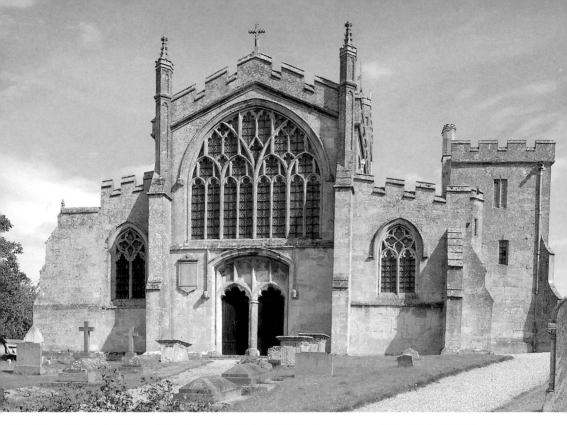

The Priory Church of St Mary, St Katharine and All Saints, Edington (above and below left), is the finest surviving example of a collegiate church in southern England. St Mary the Virgin in Steeple Ashton is another splendid Wiltshire church (below right).

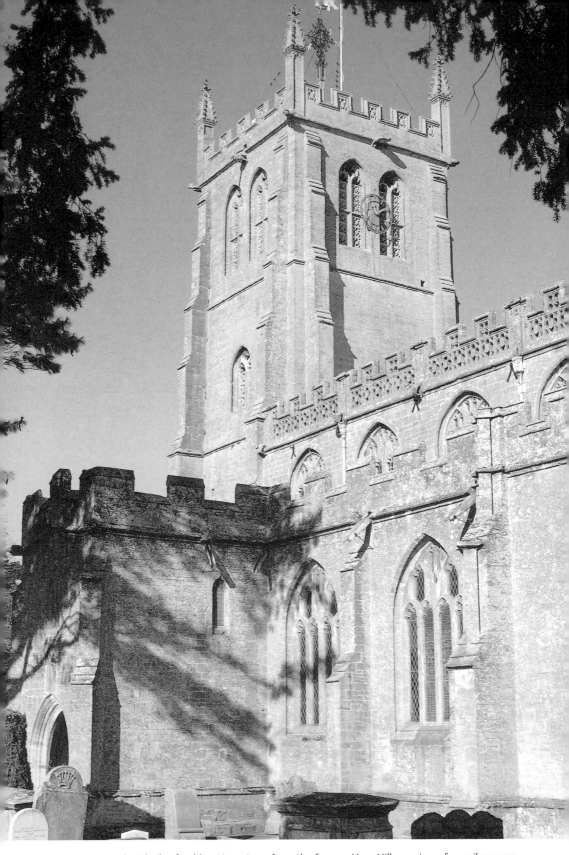

All Saints, Martock, is built of golden Ham stone from the famous Ham Hill quarries a few miles away.

St Cuthbert holds the head of King Oswald which joined him in his shrine at Durham after the king's death at the battle of Masserfield in 642. On the south side of the tower are displayed the badges of Edward IV: a falcon standing on a fetterlock and a rose below a royal crown with a lion standing on it.

The south–west doorway is Norman, as its sumptuous carving shows, and it's reckoned by many to be the most richly decorated Norman example in Yorkshire. There's a Norman doorway in the south side of the chancel as well.

As Pevsner describes it, 'The whole church has a feeling of generous space and the breathing of high, clean air', due in part to the lovely windows of the *clerestory* and the large ones at either end of the church.

Fishlake has an attractive mid-14th-century font decorated with carved figures on its eight sides including St Cuthbert (again holding King Oswald's head), Sts Wilfrid and William (Archbishops of York), St John of Beverley and St Hugh of Lincoln. Below the bowl angels hold babies in their arms.

There is some lovely Decorated work in the chancel, in particular the east window, and the chancel also contains the oldest wood in the church: the priest's stall and the front choir-stall on the north side, which are dated 1616.

St Wulfram, Grantham, Lincolnshire

According to Pevsner, 'Many connoisseurs of English parish churches would list Grantham in their first dozen', and with its superb west front and cathedral-like proportions St Wulfram's amply justifies its reputation as one of the crowning glories of English Gothic architecture.

Seen from a distance the exquisite tower and spire reflect some of the very best work of the 14th century in England. Almost equal in height to the tower, the spire rises to an apex 282 feet above the ground, making it the sixth highest in the country and the third highest among English parish churches. (Its great height has frequently been its downfall, however, for several times in its history the spire has been struck by lightning, causing serious damage in many cases.)

Taken together with the west end of the church this façade of St Wulfram's is remarkably striking and impressive – remarkable as well since so few of the elements within it are actually in proportion. The huge west windows of the two aisles differ in design and size. The tower staircase enlarges one corner of the tower and the gable ends above the windows are neither square nor centred. Nevertheless, when viewed as an ensemble, these details disappear under the soaring majesty of the overall design.

In many respects the west end of St Wulfram's embodies the nature of the whole church: it has had bits and pieces added to it down the centuries, has undergone changes in style and use, been worked on by hundreds of different craftsmen from the Middle Ages to the present and yet still manages to present an overall impression of unity and harmony.

The plan of the church shows that it is shaped as a rectangle, on the inside anyway. The outside line is broken by the north and south porches and the *chantry* chapel of St Katharyn.

The beautiful Decorated north porch was added to the church at about 1330, and was directly related to the church's patron saint by providing a suitable resting-place for the display of St Wulfram's relics in its large upper room; the fact that the structure also served as a porch was a lesser consideration.

St Wulfram was a French priest, born in the middle of the 7th century, who took to being a missionary in middle age and sailed off to Friesland to convert the pagan Friesians. Among his many achievements was the miraculous saving of children condemned as sacrifices to pagan gods. After spending twenty years there he returned to Fontenelle Abbey near Rouen, where he died in 720.

How his relics ended up in Grantham is a little uncertain. It seems likely that they may have been brought from France in the wake of the Norman Conquest as a symbol of authority for the new French Abbot of Crowland, some thirty miles away to the south-west. When Crowland Abbey burned down the relics are believed to have been moved to Grantham, where an important Saxon church already existed.

St Wulfram's weren't the only relics to go on display; those belonging to St Symphorian the Martyr and King Edgar's daughter St Etritha were also there to attract pilgrims, who formed a steady flow throughout the Middle Ages and whose alms made an important contribution to the building fund. It's revealing that the roadway north of the church was once known as Alms Lane.

The south porch is a bit of an enigma, containing several pieces of earlier structures like re-cut Norman stones or stone coffins, reset when the porch was constructed in its present shape in the middle of the 14th century. Above it a small room was created to accommodate the custodian of the church's treasures and the holy relics, which could be seen across the church behind a grille in the north wall. Since 1598 this room has housed St Wulfram's chained library, donated by Francis Trigge, Rector of Welbourn, for 'the better increasing of learninge and knowledge of divinitie and other liberall sciences'. Eighty-three of the books still have their chains attached.

St Katharyn's Chapel was the last of the three external extensions to be added to the church, built as a private chapel for the wool-merchant Thomas Hall and his family; his coat of arms is still clearly visible above the doorway that leads into what is now the vestry.

The medieval wool trade and the wool-merchants who established chantry chapels brought about the great building programme that transformed St Wulfram's into the magnificent parish church it is today. The north wall was built in the middle of the 13th century, with windows in the Early English style. The south wall followed during the course of the next century. Once the new building was roofed, the walls of the old Norman church were dismantled revealing the vast new interior for the first time. Not long after, work began on the Lady chapel, built above two vaulted crypts that were originally only accessible from the churchyard.

The last portion of the church's rectangular plan to be constructed was the Corpus Christi chapel, built in the middle of the 15th century for the Guild of Corpus

Christi which formed the earliest administrative body in Grantham.

As a church liberally endowed by wealthy benefactors, St Wulfram's suffered severely from the reforming zeal of the 16th century. What it gained in its library it lost in its stone *rood screen*, its vestments and church plate, and its pictures, statuary and other works of art. The shrine of St Wulfram disappeared from parish records as well.

The church then became increasingly cluttered in the succeeding centuries until Gilbert Scott was engaged to report on the state of the building, and subsequently to undertake a programme of restoration that returned it to something like its former Gothic splendour.

Among the more unusual things to see inside are the charity boards on display, one of which details the bequest of forty shillings a year to the Angel Inn by one Michael Solomon. This sum was to be paid in return for a sermon preached in St Wulfram's against the sin of drunkenness. It was used to great effect when the temperance movements were at their height during the last century, though more mellow references to the perils of drink have been made in the Solomon Bequest sermons of recent years.

St Oswald, Grasmere, Cumbria

The Lakeland village of Grasmere and the poet William Wordsworth are inseparably linked. Here Wordsworth spent fourteen of his most creative years, and he and the closest members of his family are buried in St Oswald's churchyard.

The church is dedicated to the Northumbrian king who was killed in battle near Hexham in the year 642, fighting Penda, the heathen king of Mercia. Local tradition holds that the saint preached on the very spot where the church now stands and, although nothing in the present building pre-dates the 13th century, evidence suggests that it was preceded by two others.

In the fifth book of the *Excursion* Wordsworth described the interior:

> Not raised in nice proportion was the pile,
> But large and massy; for duration built;
> With pillars crowded, and the roof upheld
> By naked rafters intricately crossed,
> Like leafless underboughs in some thick wood,
> All withered by the depth of shade above.

On entering the church today you will still find its interior impressive. The roof especially catches the eye, as Wordsworth implies. His 'naked rafters intricately crossed' are the result of an ingenious solution to the problem faced around the turn of the 16th century, when the church needed to be enlarged to cater for the growing congregation in the large parish of Grasmere.

The original St Oswald's consisted of the nave and tower alone. Alongside this nave, a new nave was built on the north side, only a yard shorter and with its own pitched roof. The original north wall of the church was pierced in five places to create 'arches' joining the two. However, rain and snow collected in the gully between the two roofs, and in 1562 work began to construct a new roof spanning both naves. To do this, the builders built a second tier of arches on the old north wall to carry the timbers that would bring the whole church under one roof. Thus a two-storeyed arcade was created, with a design of roof timbers unlike any other in the country.

The flagstone floor of St Oswald's was laid in 1841. Until that time the floor, like that of the majority of other country churches, had consisted of bare earth strewn with rushes to keep out the cold and damp. Around this practical measure developed the tradition of 'rushbearing', ancient in origin (possibly pre-Christian), and still kept alive in Grasmere and a few other parishes in the North, in spite of the installation of more effective methods of keeping out the chill.

In days gone by the rushbearers themselves were rewarded for their efforts, which were usually performed on or close to the patronal festival; in the case of St Oswald this is 5 August. Today the rushes are spread discreetly in the church, before the actual Rushbearing ceremony, on the Saturday nearest that date. Pride of place now goes to the various 'bearings', traditional decorations made of rushes and flowers that symbolize various religious and historical themes. These same patterns are used year after year, lovingly redecorated for each Rushbearing, and often carried by members of the same families from one generation to the other.

The symbolic bearing of the rushes themselves is performed by six Rush Maidens, who carry rushes on a finely woven white cloth in front of the procession of 'bearings'. From the church the full procession, led by the choir and clergy carrying sprays of rushes, walks through the village before returning to the church for a special service. After this the 'bearings' are left by the altar and their bearers are rewarded with the traditional piece of gingerbread stamped with St Oswald's name.

William Wordsworth planted eight of the yew trees in the churchyard in 1819. One of them casts its shadow over the grave simply marked 'William Wordsworth 1850. Mary Wordsworth 1859.' where the poet and his wife were laid to rest. His sister Dorothy, whose diaries shed so much light on her brother's life, lies buried close by, as do his children Catharine, Thomas and Dora. Coleridge's son Hartley is there, too, in a grave said to have been chosen by Wordsworth.

The small building by the lych-gate, formerly the village school, has since 1854 been the home of 'Sarah Nelson's Original Celebrated Grasmere Gingerbread' which is baked here according to a traditional recipe. That, too, is well worth a visit.

St Mary the Virgin, Great Warley, Essex

2 MILES SOUTH-WEST OF BRENTWOOD, ON B186

There are two Essex churches in this collection, both at either end of the history of English church-building. St Andrew's at Greensted (which follows on page 130) is one of the very oldest churches included, St Mary's at Great Warley the youngest. As such, it is a very good example of Art Nouveau architecture and design from the opening years of this century.

The story of the church begins in 1876 with the arrival in Great Warley of a wealthy and philanthropic stockbroker named Evelyn Heseltine. He set up home with his young family and gradually established an estate of almost feudal proportions and influence which culminated in the building of a new parish church to replace the crumbling building that had served the congregation for six hundred years.

The foundation stone was laid in 1902 by Evelyn Heseltine's wife, in conjunction with the celebrations of Edward VII's coronation that year. The architect appointed to draw up the plans was Harrison Townsend, while the interior features and decoration were entrusted to the noted sculptor and designer Sir William Reynolds-Stephens.

Externally the church resembles many in the county with a belfry and *broach* spire clad with wooden shingles, a design commonly found in Essex. The major exception in the design was the choice of an *apse* at the east end.

In his design Reynolds-Stephens's principal objective had been to direct the worshippers' attention towards the figure of the risen Christ in the centre of the *reredos*. Since there is no great east window to distract you, his objective is achieved in a *triptych* at the centre of which is the panel showing Christ standing on a serpent and raising his hand in blessing. Bronze, silver gilt, marble, enamel and mother-of-pearl are all used in the design, and the two flanking panels of ormolu show the Nativity on the left hand and Christ's Entombment on the right.

This blend of materials is seen throughout the church fittings, and forms an intriguing contrast with almost every other church described here. The font comes closest to others in being fashioned from marble, both black and white. Its design is unmistakably Art Nouveau, however, as is the cover made from metal inlaid with mussel pearl. The pulpit is cruciform in shape and constructed from a variety of metals joined by rivets that are themselves employed to decorative effect. There is metalwork in the lectern too, inlaid with pearlesque shell and mounted on a plinth of black marble.

The *rood screen* is worked in brass, mounted on a low wall of dark green marble from which climb brass rose trees with enamel fruits and flowers of mother-of-pearl. In contrast, the screen separating the side chapel from the nave is carved from walnut, following a design of poppy plants with pewter flowers.

Up above, the wagon vault roof is made from plain boarding with broad ribs of rose trees flowering in circular clusters presented in low relief. The walls are covered with natural stucco plaster, interspersed by low-relief panels decorated with lilies. The framework of these panels, and the flowers and fruit details in the church, are the only places where paint has been applied. In every other case the materials employed lend their own colouring, in accordance with the Art Nouveau principle of accepting materials as they are and formulating design from their inherent properties.

Like it or loathe it, a visit to Great Warley church offers examples of a distinctive decorative style that reflects the age that spawned it just as graphically as any medieval one.

St Michael, Great Witley, Hereford and Worcester

St Michael's was once the church of Witley Court, the great estate of the Foley family. Today the house it served stands a gaunt and burnt-out ruin, but St Michael's remains as a confident reminder of the grandeur of the Lords Foley who brought it into being.

On the site of an older and very dilapidated parish church, this church was built in the two years from 1733, when the first Lord Foley died, to 1735, when his wife died, only a short time before St Michael's was consecrated. A dozen years later their son, the second Lord Foley, took advantage of the financial predicament of the second Duke of Chandos; his debts had forced him to sell the fabulous family seat of Canons, near Edgware, and Lord Foley bought the chapel windows and ceiling to be installed at Great Witley. The result is that St Michael's has an interior of remarkable exuberance for an English country church.

The ten round-headed baroque windows brought from Canons were painted by Joshua Price, after designs by Sebastian Ricci, and show a variety of religious subjects.

The walls and ceiling are a riot of white and gold plasterwork, possibly the work of Pietro Bagutti (who had decorated the interior of St Martin-in-the-Fields). The coved ceiling from the chapel at Canons is an equally flamboyant display of embossed panels and elaborate scrollwork that forms a backdrop to three paintings attributed to the Venetian artist, Antonio Bellucci. The largest of these, in the centre, shows the Ascension, the smaller one to the west the Nativity, while that on the eastern side shows the Descent from the Cross.

A further feature brought to Great Witley from Canons was the organ casing above the balustraded organ loft. In its original setting this housed the organ on which Handel played and composed when he was in charge of music for the Chandos household for several years.

In 1862 the first Earl of Dudley undertook a number of alterations of his own. Externally he encased the church in stone. Inside he removed the old box pews and replaced them with mock Gothic ones, which nevertheless blend with the grandiose extravagances of the interior.

St Andrew, Greensted, Essex

Greensted is a small, well-wooded hamlet only a couple of miles from the eastern terminus of London's Central Line at Ongar; the name Greensted means a clearing in the wood. There is known to have been at least one previous church on the site, and it's likely that this was founded on a Celtic pre-Christian place of worship.

After several attempts to convert Essex, Christianity finally arrived in 654 when Sigbert, a recently converted Saxon king, invited St Cedd to sail south from the monastery at Lindisfarne, off the Northumbrian coast, to build a Christian outpost and lead a mission in his kingdom. Two centuries later, in 845, Saxon craftsmen built the present church of St Andrew at Greensted.

It was a simple building measuring thirty feet long by ten wide. The roof was thatched. The walls were made from huge oak logs split vertically, tongued and grooved to keep out the draughts, and held in place in their oak sill by wooden pegs. There were no windows; holes bored in the walls gave some ventilation and rush torches dipped in mutton fat provided artificial light. The fire risk they posed, and their smell, can only be imagined. Nevertheless St Andrew's is still standing, making it the oldest surviving example of a Saxon timber-framed church and the oldest wooden church in the world. (After 1100 years its oak walls are so hard it's practically impossible to drive a nail into the timber.)

Over the centuries there have been several additions to the original Saxon structure. At the turn of the 16th century, during the reign of Henry VII, the chancel was rebuilt, three dormer windows were added, the thatch was replaced by tiles and the porch was constructed.

At probably the same time the little shingled tower, again made entirely of wood, was added. Timber towers like St Andrew's are a particular feature of churches in this part of Essex. They rise straight from the ground, supported independently from the nave and braced by beams set at an angle to the upright corner posts. Crude as these structures may sound, they're surprisingly robust. During the Second World War a flying bomb fell only a few yards from a similar tower at Navestock, five miles south of Greensted, and failed to topple it.

In spite of some fairly drastic restoration in 1847–8, which included the replacement of the three Tudor dormers by six Victorian ones, and more elaborate roof trusses for the simple tie-beams that preceded them, the church's timbered interior manages to retain its warmth and sense of great age. Traces of torch burns still mark the walls and up in the west end is a stained-glass window depicting the head of St Edmund, the only piece of original 14th-century stained glass in the church. The rest was stolen and somehow ended up in Australia; it was sent back to Greensted on board a ship that unfortunately sank during the homeward voyage, taking the glass from St Andrew's with it to the bottom.

There is another Australian connection dating from the last century, associated with the infamous treatment of the Tolpuddle Martyrs during the 1830s. Such a hue and cry in England followed their transportation to Australia for seven years, essentially for forming a trade union to achieve better pay and working conditions for farm labourers, that after three years their sentences were commuted, in 1837.

Prevented from returning to their homes in Dorset through the opposition of the county's farmers, the six 'martyrs' were given farm tenancies in Greensted and High Laver, a few miles to the north. The register in St Andrew's records the marriage of James Brine, one of the six, to Elizabeth Standfield, daughter of one of the other 'martyrs', in 1839. The ending to the story is not entirely happy, however, because local opposition soon forced them overseas again, to Canada this time, where they settled in the province of Ontario.

St Edmund, who is commemorated in the north-east window, was a martyr in the more conventional sense and as such became the first patron saint of England, before the Normans substituted St George. Edmund was king in this part of the country and was put to death by the Danes in AD 870, thirty-five years after St Andrew's had been built. His body was enshrined in the town we now call Bury St Edmunds, but was later removed to protect it from further Danish attacks. By 1013, when fighting with the invaders had subsided, it was decided to restore the saint to his resting-place. On the way there, his body rested in the little wooden church in the clearing at Greensted.

St Mary, Sompting, retains its Saxon tower, capped with a four-sided shingled roof that is the closest Saxon builders came to erecting a spire.

St Nicholas, Barfreston (above), is a fine Norman church known for its beautifully worked stone carving, while the intriguing exterior of St Augustine's church, not far away in Brookland (below), tempts the visitor inside to view the unusual circular lead font.

St Mary, Stoke D'Abernon, has retained much of its original Saxon structure.

St Mark and St Luke, Avington, standing alone among trees, has kept its original Norman plan.

All Saints, Hawton, Nottinghamshire

In the Middle Ages, Hawton was a much larger village than the small hamlet the visitor finds today. Domesday Book records two churches, on the site of one of which Sir Roger de Compton began building the nave and north aisle of the present church that he dedicated to All Saints. This work dates from the 1280s and forms the oldest part of the building.

In 1325 Hawton's glorious chancel was built with its superb east window, one of the finest curvilinear east windows in the country from this period. On the south side are richly carved *sedilia* and double *piscina*, the former showing the figures of several saints, including St Peter, St Nicholas and St Edward the Martyr. You can also spot a couple of men down on all fours gathering grapes among the foliage, and a pelican sitting in her nest, a fairly common Christian motif.

To the left of the founder's tomb on the north side of the chancel is a doorway that led into a side chapel (now demolished) that acted as a hermitage in the Middle Ages, and the squint hole that gave the hermit sight of the main altar can still be seen. And to the right stands the church's most famous treasure, the intricately carved Easter sepulchre. For a village church the quality and detail of its workmanship is remarkable.

Easter sepulchres acted as the resting place for the reserved sacrament between mass on Maundy Thursday and Easter morning, recalling Christ's statement at the Last Supper that he would not drink 'of the fruit of the vine until that day that I drink it new in the kingdom of God', to quote St Mark. The decoration therefore shows scenes from the story of the Resurrection. Down at the bottom are four Roman soldiers, dressed in armour but fast asleep. In the middle section is the risen Christ, still carrying the grave clothes. To the right stand Mary Magdalene, Mary, the mother of James, and Salome who went to the tomb to anoint the body and found it gone. In the top of the sepulchre stand the disciples looking upwards and right at the very top are Christ's feet ascending into heaven.

Hawton church is also notable for its noble 15th-century tower that still has its original door inscribed with the signs of the Zodiac.

St Andrew, Heckington, Lincolnshire

St Andrew's, Heckington is the third church to have been built on the site, although no trace remains of the predecessors of the famous cruciform building that has long been admired as one of the finest Decorated churches in the country.

One of the most appealing features of St Andrew's is its continuity of design. The masons' marks that are seen all over the church indicate that the same craftsmen who started work were still there when the finishing touches were made, and since they packed their tools and left little has been added or altered.

The one exception is the Puritan destruction of the statues and other decorative features in the 16th and 17th centuries, but even so Heckington is still richly decorated with eighty carved *corbels* and 198 gargoyles, not to mention the pinnacles. Even the buttresses carried niches in which sat a total of thirty-eight statues, of which only the one representing St John survives in the extreme south–west buttress. There are heads and figures at the apex of every gable in addition to a profusion of *crockets*. Octagonal turrets with carved heads at every angle stand at the east end of both the nave and chancel.

Rising above these are the tower and spire, reaching a height just short of 186 feet.

Pevsner regarded Lincolnshire as the best county for

135

Decorated work and among a rich feast of external displays the south porch at Heckington ranks among the very best. The porch has two projecting double buttresses with canopied niches that once accommodated now-missing statues. Between the arch and the pointed apex Christ is seen, seated above a design of angels carrying censers and a shield bearing the arms of Richard II. At the bases of the arch are two shields decorated with the royal coats of arms of Edward the Confessor (on the left) and St Edmund (on the right).

The nave of St Andrew's is as high as the combined width of the nave and aisles, which provides a pleasing symmetry. The transepts come west of the easternmost bay of the nave, forming an unusual ante-chancel, in the floor of which is an equally unusual tomb inscribed with the T-shaped cross of St Anthony.

In the north side of the chancel wall lies the tomb of Richard Potesgrave, vicar of the church and sometime chaplain to Edward II and Edward III, who spent some of the wealth acquired from these royal positions in decorating the chancel at Heckington. The *sedilia* display some of the best carving in the church, with figures of Christ and his mother, together with other saints, attended by angels and watched over by grotesque figures of men and women in a range of activities from eating to enjoying a good quarrel.

Heckington's other great treasure is its Easter sepulchre, similar in design and identical in function to the one at Hawton in Nottinghamshire (described on page 133). A plaster cast of the Heckington Easter sepulchre was put on display in the Great Exhibition of 1851. Brackets in the wall on either side were used to support the Lenten veil that covered the sepulchre during Lent.

The wonderfully light tracery in the east window is another feature that establishes Heckington's claim as a supreme example of the Decorated period. During the time when the church had a flat-pitched roof following restoration work in the 15th century, both this tracery and the chancel arch were exposed to the elements on both sides, though fortunately neither appears to have suffered unduly.

St Augustine, Hedon, Humberside

Widely known as the 'King of Holderness', St Augustine's is both a fascinating record of the changes in church architecture that came about during the three hundred years it was under construction, from the 12th to the 15th centuries, and an equally vivid record of the history of Hedon.

In the latter half of the 12th century, during the reign of Henry II, Hedon was the most important shipping centre on the north bank of the River Humber, thanks to Hedon Haven and a system of canals that brought ships to the town, establishing it as an important trading centre. The design of St Augustine's was conceived to complement this mercantile prosperity, and work began confidently around 1200.

However, the emergence of the port of Kingston-upon-Hull that steadily drew trade away from Hedon, coupled with the ravages of the Black Death, meant that the original designs had to be constantly modified to match the diminishing funds available for the church. All the same, the building was completed and although less opulently decorated than originally planned, it is still one of the most distinguished churches in the north of England.

The south transept was the first part to be built, probably on the site of an earlier church. The south wall had to be completely rebuilt during Victorian restoration work, but the integrity of the Early English work has been largely retained. The north transept is very little altered and has beautifully worked dog-tooth decoration around the doorway and *lancet* windows. The stairways in both transepts originally led up to the wall passages that were open to the interior by archways. These passages may have once been connected to those around the chancel, though this is no longer the case.

In the chancel the windows in the *clerestory* of the north give light on to the wall passage there and below them are three lancet windows. Two other lancet windows decorated with dog-tooth designs stand at the east end of what was once the outer south wall. The filled-in arches once opened into the now demolished chantry of St Mary's.

Through the doorway in the chancel lies the 15th-century vestry which was originally built with two storeys, the upper one serving as store-room for civil and church records for several hundred years. There is a lovely lancet window in the west wall of the vestry on which is also hung one of the last surviving representations of the royal arms of Elizabeth I with the lion and dragon, issued to churches throughout the kingdom as confirmation of her position as Supreme Head of the Church in England.

The 14th century was well advanced by the time work started on building the nave. Hedon's fortunes were on the decline, and the work could only progress as funds and labour permitted. Yet progress it did, with the construction of graceful pillars supporting arches above the apex of which stand double-light clerestory windows. The aisle windows are much admired, and so is the exterior masonry of the doorways situated in both aisles.

The western end of the church was built in the Perpendicular style, many years after construction started on the eastern end of the nave.

The central tower of St Augustine's is reckoned to be the best built in the old county of Yorkshire. It stands 129 feet high, finely decorated with large belfry windows and sixteen small delicate pinnacles, calling attention to this handsome church that proudly retains something of the bygone glory of medieval Hedon.

St Andrew, Hexham,
Northumberland

Christians have worshipped in Hexham since 674, the
year in which St Wilfrid, Bishop of York, built the first
church on land given to him by Queen Ethelreda (also
spelt Etheldreda), wife of Ecgfrith (also spelt Egfrid), King
of Northumbria. The building he erected was one of the
most important in England at that time. Only four other
churches in the country had been built in stone and it's
thought that Wilfrid brought craftsmen from Rome to
help with its construction. As the saint's biographer
recorded, '. . .we have never heard of its like this side
of the Alps'.

From Rome St Wilfrid also obtained relics of St Andrew
during a visit made as part of his monastic training.
These were placed in the crypt at Hexham and soon
began attracting pilgrims. The abbey grew, acquiring
fine buildings and works of religious art, all of which
were destroyed in the Viking raids of the 9th century.
Almost nothing of the original foundation was known
to have survived; however, in 1725, workmen excavating
foundations for a buttress to strengthen the tower discovered the ancient crypt where St Andrew's relics and those
of other saints would once have lain.

As the oldest and most moving part of the present
church, this reveals a great deal about the the materials

141

and design St Wilfrid would have had at his disposal. In shape the crypt at Hexham is similar to that built below the *apse* at St Peter's in Rome at the very beginning of the 5th century. The walls are constructed almost entirely of stone bearing the signs of Roman tooling, and probably taken from the ruins of the Roman fort at Corbridge, three miles away on the other side of the River Tyne. Originally two passages led into the crypt and its antechamber: a south passage for the monks, and the north one for pilgrims who would have viewed the precious relics through a grille. Passing through this north passage they would have seen a Roman altar cut to form an arch-head in the roof, one of the several distinctive pieces of Roman work to be found in the abbey.

Among other reminders of St Wilfrid's church is the 'frith stool', or sanctuary chair that now stands in the choir on the site of the original apse. More decorated than the one at Beverley (described on page 29) this was also carved from a single block of stone at the end of the 7th century. When first installed in St Andrew's it would have been placed in the apse as the bishop's seat, surrounded by benches on the walls of the apse, where the other clergy would have sat. In medieval times fugitives could claim sanctuary within one mile of the frith stool and crosses (still remembered in the names of White Cross and Maiden Cross) marked the boundary line until the rights of privilege were eventually abolished by James I in 1624.

In a niche in the south choir aisle is a small Saxon chalice that was found in a coffin unearthed during more digging work in 1860. Although it can't be accurately dated, this is reckoned to be the oldest chalice in England and would probably have been carried by the monks as they travelled around the country administering the sacraments. The font is ancient, too, consisting of a large circular bowl that may be of Roman origin, decorated hundreds of years later with 13th-century dog-tooth design topped by a canopy carved in 1916 in the style of Jacobean work.

After the Viking and Norman destruction, Hexham Abbey lay in ruins until the beginning of the 12th century when the Archbishop of York established an Augustinian priory and built a new church on the site of St Wilfrid's abbey, following the Early English style of the period. This, too, suffered from Scottish attacks in the late 13th century which left the priory a smouldering ruin. Traces of lead that ran from the flaming roof can still be seen around the church in cracks in the stonework. As a result of this damage, the Augustinian canons closed off the nave by walling up the arch leading into it from the crossing. From then on the chancel and transepts served both the priory and the parish, so that when the priory was suppressed and its other buildings allowed to fall into disrepair at the Dissolution of the Monasteries, the church was able to survive, in rather diminished circumstances. In fact it wasn't until 1905 that work began on rebuilding the nave on the plan of the 13th-century one, with a single aisle on the north side.

Entry to the church today is through a vaulted passage known as a *slype*, that lies at the southern end of the south transept. Ahead is the north transept, distinguished by its tall *lancet* windows and richly decorated east aisle that was once divided into small chapels.

In addition to the slype, the south transept contains another feature unique to Hexham that dramatically recalls the life of the priory that flourished here during the Middle Ages – the night stairs. Down these the canons would process from their dormitory into the church for their night-time offices, which began at about two in the morning. Today the choir follow their footsteps from the Song School as they make their way down to each service.

The large Saxon cross shaft in the south transept is thought to be that erected at the head of the grave of St Acca, and was carved in the middle of the 8th century with a distinctive decoration of vine-scroll tracery. The smaller shaft is possibly the one that stood at the foot of St Acca's grave.

The other ancient monument standing in this transept is the Roman tombstone at the foot of the night stairs. This is the memorial stone to a twenty-five-year-old standard bearer named Flavinius who died while stationed on Hadrian's wall in the first century AD. He's shown mounted on horseback, dressed in full armour with helmet and plume and carrying the standard. Below him is the crouching figure of a Briton holding an oval shield and brandishing a sword pointing upwards as if to lunge at horse or rider. In the detail of the carving, old as it is, you get a vivid, dramatic glimpse of early English history.

The first part of the priory church to be built was the chancel, dating from 1180, and decorated with some distinctive Early English *stiff-leaf* work. There are some splendidly carved 15th-century *misericords* decorated with a variety of subjects that include a vampire, a Green Man with foliage sprouting from his mouth and a wyvern (a two-footed dragon).

More 15th-century woodwork can be found in the sanctuary where there is a lectern with fourteen painted panels showing Christ, the Virgin Mary and the twelve Apostles. Behind this stands a painted *reredos* that shows seven of the twelve bishops of Hexham. Below these are four panels depicting the medieval allegory known as the Dance of Death, in which Death – represented by a skeleton – is shown dancing with a cardinal, a king, an emperor and a pope. This served to remind the congregation that the same end awaits us all, irrespective of our status on earth. It was a theme common in the Middle

Ages, but the paintings at Hexham are the most vivid example that survived the Reformation.

Prior Leschman's *chantry* chapel in the north choir aisle contains the best carving in the church, in which local masons have created some fascinating caricatures of human attributes like gluttony, piety, purity, penitence and vanity together with St George and his dragon, musicians, a jester and a border raider carrying off a sheep. There is also a painted reredos showing the Resurrection and instruments of Christ's Passion.

The *rood screen* at the crossing, erected by Thomas Smithson, prior from 1491 to 1524, has both carved tracery and painted figures representing the bishops of both Hexham and Lindisfarne. This is the only closed wooden screen with a loft that survives in a former English monastic church and confirms Hexham's pre-eminent status as one of the most interesting – as well as historic – churches in the whole country.

St Mary the Virgin, Holy Island, Northumberland

10 MILES SOUTH OF BERWICK-UPON-TWEED, OFF A1 BY
CAUSEWAY THAT FLOODS AT HIGH TIDE

As its name suggests, Holy Island is famed as the birth-
place of English Christianity. In the year 635 St Aidan
arrived here from the island of Iona, off the west coast
of Scotland, coming at the invitation of King Oswald
who wanted him to teach Christianity to the Angles of
Northumbria. Lindisfarne Monastery was built here, and
for two and a half centuries was one of the seedbeds of the
early faith in northern England before it was destroyed by
Danish invaders in 875. The beautiful Lindisfarne Gospels,
now housed in the British Museum, were compiled here
at the beginning of the 8th century and are recalled in the
designs on the embroidered kneelers and carpet in front
of the altar of the present church.

After destruction by the Danes, the island remained
deserted until the 11th century when Benedictine monks
from Durham returned to build a priory, the red sandstone
ruins of which still stand immediately to the east of the
church.

Work on the priory began in 1093, using stone quarried
on the mainland and brought over to the island on ox-
drawn carts. The ruined pillars of the nave retain enough
detail to show that they and the rest of the priory church
were almost certainly the work of the same builders, or

146

school of builders, who built Durham Cathedral. Like that cathedral, the priory church at Lindisfarne was built with an *apse*, but both were rebuilt with square ends in the 12th century.

Two centuries later border wars were fought between the English and the Scots and, situated as it was close to the fighting zone, the priory at Lindisfarne was fortified in several places; the slits in the walls were created as crossbow-loops for the defenders. As it turned out, Scottish invaders never arrived; but the crossbow-loops remind us of those troubled times.

The priory at Holy Island was never large, probably housing fewer than a dozen monks at any one time, which made it a prime target for Henry VIII's commissioners in 1537. Once it was dissolved the buildings fell into disrepair. The lead was stripped from the roof and loaded on to a ship to be taken away – then sank to the sea bottom when she foundered. Much of the building stone was also taken from the priory to build the castle that overlooks the small harbour.

While all this was going on, however, the parish church was standing as a silent witness as it had done since Norman times. Although dating from the late 13th century, it has a fine Norman chancel arch, the oldest surviving part of the church.

The long chancel, like most of the church, is Early English in style. The *reredos* behind the altar shows figures of the saints who brought Christianity to these northern lands. The diamond-shaped coats of arms known as *hatchments* belong to the local families of Selby, Askew and Hagerston and date from the 18th and 19th centuries. The carpet in front of the altar is based on one of the so-called 'carpet pages' taken from the Lindisfarne Gospel according to St Mark. Copies of these Gospels and the Book of Kells, which some think may have been compiled on Holy Island as well, are displayed in a case in the south aisle.

147

The north aisle is the fishermen's aisle, where the island's fishermen traditionally sit when they come to church. The altar cloth shows two fish, between which is the Greek word for 'a fish', which has been a Christian symbol since earliest times. Several of Jesus' disciples were fishermen, of course, among them St Peter, and the altar in the north aisle is used for Holy Communion on St Peter's Day (29 June), a fitting reminder of the early beginnings of the faith which first took root in England on this very spot.

St Wendreda was very much a saint of the eastern counties and this splendid church in March was dedicated
to her in 1343, three hundred years after her death.

St Andrew, Greensted (below), is one of the oldest churches in this collection while St Mary the Virgin, Great Warley (above), also in Essex, is one of the youngest.

St Peter, Howden, Humberside

St Peter's is a large cruciform church with a tall central tower that rises magnificently over the market town of Howden. The minster today presents two contrasting faces, the nave and transepts with the tower between them which form the present parish church, and the ruined east end, chancel and chapter house that was once the focal point of the collegiate church that was establish by the Prior of Durham in 1267.

The major part of the present church was built in the late 13th and early 14th centuries. Moving westwards from the tower, the style gradually changes from Early English to Decorated.

After the minster had achieved collegiate status, ambitious plans were laid for rebuilding the nave and choir. The nave was completed at the turn of the 14th century, the choir some time between 1320 and 1340. Since the choir belonged to the canons serving in the college, greater emphasis was placed on its overall design and decoration – as the many niches for statues on the exterior implies.

The canons of Howden set to work once again towards the end of the 14th century, constructing the beautiful octagonal chapter house (the last of this shape to be built in England) which served as their official meeting-place.

They enjoyed the use of this for a little over a century and a half. Since it wasn't a monastery, Howden was

149

spared the destruction meted out to those religious houses by Henry VIII, but in 1548 collegiate churches and chantries went the same way and Howden's wealth passed to the Crown, and subsequently from Elizabeth I to local gentry.

The nave remained in use as the parish church but the choir that the canons had so cherished fell into disrepair, the new owners declining to spend any more on its maintenance. By 1609 the congregation gave up any hope of saving the choir as a place of worship and blocked it off; thereafter the nave alone was used. Throughout the 17th century the condition of choir and chapter house gradually deteriorated. First the lead was taken from the roof to patch the roof of the nave. Then Parliamentarian troops stabled their horses in the choir and north transept one night in 1644 and did a considerable amount of damage to the tombs and other monuments. The end of the choir finally came during a thunderstorm on the feast of St Michael and All Angels (29 September) 1696, when the roof and its wonderful stone vaulting caved in. Fifty-four years later, on Boxing Day 1750, the roof of the chapter house collapsed as well.

As it stands today, the minster is really only two thirds of its original length. The nave, which measures just under 108 feet from end to end, was divided from the choir, a couple of feet longer, by the *pulpitum* (a stone *rood screen*). Today this forms the focal point at the east end of the church and in the archway that originally led into the choir stands the chapel of St Cuthbert, where the sacrament is reserved. The pulpitum is richly decorated, with two niches on either side of the archway all canopied by delicate *tabernacle* work. There are statues in each one as well, medieval statues, though not those originally housed there. These were probably placed in the niches during the tidying-up work that took place in the ruins at the end of the 18th century. Nevertheless all four sit happily in their present surroundings, and complement the glorious work around them.

In the south transept that now serves as the Lady chapel stand a couple of items of particular interest. On the left of the altar is a rare 14th-century statue of the Blessed Virgin Mary, on whose shoulder perches a dove whispering into her ear; the bird symbolizes the Annunciation.

On the other side of the altar is a rectangular stone structure, decorated with shields, whose association with the minster is far less easily defined. It's unlikely to be an altar. It might be a tomb, and there's a possibility that it may have contained Howden's collection of relics before they disappeared with the Reformation. By 1548 these made an impressive tally. There were pieces of the crosses on which Christ and St Andrew were believed respectively to have been crucified; dust from the bones of St John the Baptist; a hand belonging to St John the Evangelist; assorted bones of St Lawrence, St Theodore, St Sebastian and St Clement; some of the Blessed Virgin Mary's hair; part of the cradle in which she apparently rocked the infant Christ; and some of the vestments worn by St Thomas the Martyr, St Leonard and St Cuthbert. Among the *chantries* established at Howden were those consecrated to several of these saints, assisted no doubt by the appropriate relic.

St Mary, Ingestre, Staffordshire

Ingestre lies in the flat meadows beside the River Trent and probably derives its name from Danish settlers who put down roots here in the 9th or 10th centuries. However, the focus of attention as far as the church is concerned lies seven or eight centuries later at the time when two members of the Chetwynd family, both named Walter, made major improvements to the estate.

In 1613 the elder Walter Chetwynd built the Hall, a fine Jacobean house, on the site of an earlier manor house. In 1671 Walter Chetwynd, his grandson, sought permission from the Archbishop of Canterbury to replace the existing medieval parish church, which was by then derelict, with a brand-new church to be built entirely at his own expense. It took a couple of years for full authorization to be given but when it came at last, Chetwynd engaged the foremost architect of the day to design the new St Mary's. He asked Sir Christopher Wren, who, like Chetwynd, was one of the early members of the Royal Society. So it is that Ingestre possesses a Wren church, completed in 1676 and regarded as the most elaborate country church of its day.

'Enter through the circular lobby under the tower,' writes Pevsner, 'and you find yourself in a room of blissful harmony.' The dominant decorative motifs are fruit and flowers adorning the plaster-work and the carved oak panelling and screen.

152

The ceiling is typical of Wren's churches and inscribed in the plaster are the names of Gilbert and S. Hand, who may well have been members of the same Hand family engaged in quarrying stone for St Paul's Cathedral.

The pews are made from Flanders oak, as is the magnificent screen topped by the royal coat of arms. This, like the pulpit with its canopy or tester, has been attributed to Grinling Gibbons and – even if not the work of Gibbons himself – must have been undertaken by a craftsman of almost equal standing and accomplishment.

As might be expected, most of the memorials are to members of the Chetwynd family. The windows in the centre of the north and south walls were both made in the William Morris workshops, the one in the north wall having been designed by Burne-Jones, that in the south wall by Baroness Gleichen.

In addition to its associations with London churches through Sir Christopher Wren, Ingestre has a more recent utilitarian one. In 1886 The Domestic Electric Lighting Co. came up from London to install electric lighting in St Mary's. This had only appeared in the first London church three years earlier, and Ingestre seems likely to have been the first Midlands church to have been lit in this way.

St Mary and St David, Kilpeck, Hereford and Worcester

8 MILES SOUTH-WEST OF HEREFORD, OFF A465

Built of a surprisingly durable sandstone, St Mary and St David is one of the most lavishly decorated and best preserved Norman village churches in England.

In Saxon times Kilpeck lay in the troubled border country between England and Celtic Wales. The whole village was enclosed by earthworks, the remains of which can still be seen. There was a Saxon church here, too, a small portion of which is still evident in the north-east corner of the chancel where the *quoins* show typical Saxon long-and-short work.

Following the Conquest, William FitzNorman built the castle that stood at the west of the church and his grandson Hugh FitzNorman gave the land to the Benedictines of St Peter at Gloucester, who founded a priory at Kilpeck in 1135. Within the next five years the church was built and has remained barely altered since then.

In its sumptuous carving the church shows the work of the so-called Herefordshire school of sculpture at its best. A good deal of it is unique to Kilpeck, both in design and craftsmanship, and the south doorway that first catches your eye as you approach is outstanding in this respect.

Here the forces of good and evil are shown contending in carvings of vibrant and vivid detail. In the outer arch are joined medallions showing animals, birds, mythical

154

monsters, a phoenix rising from the flames and dragons, all of which have been taken as symbols of the Creation. Below in the *tympanum* is the Tree of Life, heavy with grapes. The shafts on either side of the doorway are exuberantly decorated, too, with curling monsters with protruding jaws that suggest a pronounced Scandinavian influence. On the right-hand side a human face is shown being tempted by a writhing serpent to eat the forbidden fruit of the Tree of Knowledge. Across the doorway in the left-hand capital the dragon and lion are shown locked in combat and, below, the serpent is depicted head downward, implying that the dragon (symbol of evil) had been defeated.

The left-hand column also shows two men generally regarded as Welsh warriors, in spite of their wearing headgear known as Phrygian caps. Completing their outfits they are sporting chainmail jerkins and tight trousers.

Still outside the church, the *corbel-table* is worthy of a visit in its own right. Victorian restorers removed some of the more erotic figures but there are still nearly eighty grotesque carvings running right round the church, only two of which have any direct religious connection. These are the representations of the Holy Lamb of God which appear over the south doorway and at the centre of the *apse* at the east end. The others include deer, wild boar, falcons, horses, bears and the amusing pairing of a dog and rabbit. Among the human subjects are wrestlers, musicians, lovers and lots of human heads. A telephoto camera lens or a pair of binoculars helps to bring out the sheer sense of fun embodied in these beautifully carved figures.

The other feature that must be seen on the outside of the church is the wonderfully carved window, high up in the west end, decorated with intricately worked interlacing. On the same wall are two gargoyles carved as crocodile heads which are so strikingly Scandinavian

155

in appearance that they bear closest resemblance to the prows of Viking long-ships.

The interior is every bit as rewarding as the outside of the church. At the west end is a Jacobean gallery whose simple, homely design blends well with the Norman interior. Beneath this is the massive font, supported on five shafts. The font is Norman, too, though probably not the work of the Herefordshire school.

Looking eastwards the nave, chancel and apse diminish in height and width, lending a sense of length to the church. The chancel arch is another feature unique to Kilpeck in the carvings of the saints that flank it on either side. Each jamb carries three haloed Apostles, one above the other. Below the chancel arch is an ancient holy water stoup formed from a large bowl clasped by elongated rams and standing on a base carved with snakes' heads.

The windows in the rib-vaulted apse are original, although the glass was installed during restoration work at the end of the last century.

Before leaving Kilpeck, take a look at the surrounding countryside from the top of the castle mound, which is a short walk away through the churchyard. You can get a good view from here across to the brooding hills of Wales.

St Cuthbert, Kirkleatham, Cleveland

The name 'Kirkleatham' means 'the church on the hill-side' and in spite of the Georgian origin of the present building, there has been a church on the site of St Cuthbert's since the 9th century. As was the case at Fishlake, near Doncaster, the church took its name and patronage from the peregrinations of St Cuthbert's body at the end of the 10th century, which made a number of stop-overs across the north of England before finally being laid to rest in Durham Cathedral.

The core of the tower is medieval, rebuilt in 1731. The nave and chancel of the previous building were taken down in 1761 and replaced two years later by the present ones; the upper part of the tower was also rebuilt at this time. Inside the church, two rows of Tuscan columns in the nave support the roof. The oak pews were installed as tall box pews in 1763, only to be cut down to their present height a little over a century later. The handsome pulpit with its inlaid panels was similarly a fine three-decker, until that too was reduced in stature in accordance with Victorian fashion.

The chancel, and indeed the whole church, is dominated by the memory of the Turner family who settled in Kirkleatham in 1623 when John Turner, the manager of alum mines in the area, bought the manor and built a new mansion to the east of the church. His son, Sir William Turner, became a wealthy woollen draper and

157

Lord Mayor of London. He gained the friendship of Wren and Pepys, among other prominent men of the day, and acted as moneylender to Charles II. At home in Kirkleatham he built the hospital named after him, a U-shaped range of buildings with a splendid chapel that provided accommodation and education for the poor of the parish. In its nobility of conception and elegance of design the Sir William Turner Hospital reflects the influence of Wren's architecture and stands as the most impressive almshouse in the country.

Back at the church, the first Sir John Turner's great-grandson, Cholmley Turner, undertook the most prominent of its additions in 1740 when he built the octagonal baroque mausoleum on the north side of the chancel to designs by James Gibb, the architect of St Martin-in-the-Fields. His son, Marwood Turner, had died the year before at the age of twenty-two while making his 'Grand Tour' of Europe, and to his statue goes pride of place in the family mausoleum. Two other statues commemorate his father and Sir Charles Turner, the last of the family line. Sir William Turner, founder of the Hospital, lies in the large table-tomb in the centre of the floor, where it was placed after being moved from a special chapel in which the organ now stands. The mausoleum also contains two medieval coffin covers, and a small stone coffin, presumably made for a child.

St John the Baptist, St Lawrence and St Anne, Knowle, West Midlands

2 MILES SOUTH-EAST OF SOLIHULL, ON A41

Knowle is perhaps the best Perpendicular church built in Warwickshire (as it was before part of the county was incorporated into the West Midlands). It was built in the final years of the 14th century by a wealthy resident named Walter Cook, in order to save villagers like himself the long walk to the former parish church three miles away at Hampton-in-Arden. In winter the flooding of the River Blyth added further hazards to an already demanding trek.

Knowle church has historic connections with the Guild of St Anne, also founded by Walter Cook. In 1412, ten years after work on the church had been completed, he built the beautiful Guild House just to the west of the church to serve as its headquarters; today parish meetings are held downstairs, while the parish office occupies the upper storey. At the same time he enlarged the nave to accommodate the growing number of Guild members and raised the roof so that a *clerestory* could be built to let in more light. (St Anne's Cottage, which stands next to the Guild House, dates from the same time and now provides accommodation for the curate.)

The church also became a collegiate one in 1412, served by ten priests, which required the enlargement of the chancel as well. This rendered the original *sedilia* in the south wall redundant and they were hidden behind the choir-stalls, with only their tops showing. Today their replacements, positioned so high in the wall as to be unusable, don't appear to be much of an improvement, but there are sound historic reasons for this.

When the church was extended eastwards it's believed that the new east wall butted against another building, which made it impossible to pass right round the church as required by several medieval processions. The only solution was to build a processional way *underneath* the east end, just as happened at Walpole St Peter in Norfolk (described on page 253). This meant raising the floor level in the east end of the chancel, hence the logical position of the new seating arrangements. Three hundred years later, in 1745, the processional way had to be filled in since it was weakening the east end of the church and, once it had gone, there was no need for the floor level of the sanctuary to be higher then that of the rest of the church. So this was lowered to its present level, leaving the seats high and dry in the wall.

The handsome carved screen, along with the choir-stalls, dates from the 15th century.

The octagonal font in the baptistery at the other end of the nave was made in 1402. Close by stands one of the church's two chests hollowed from a single tree trunk and bound with iron, which was used to house parish records and treasures. This was originally fitted with three locks and could only be opened when both churchwardens and the minister were present with their respective keys.

Although the pulpit is modern, some sixty years old, the hour-glass on it used for timing sermons dates from 1674, although the term hour-glass is something of a misnomer in this case because the sand actually runs for only twenty minutes.

Priory of St Mary Magdalene, Lanercost, Cumbria

Lanercost Priory lies in the northern Border country. The Roman wall built during the time of the Emperor Hadrian runs close by, and provided much of the building material for the priory. In the Middle Ages it provided a resting-place for alternating English and Scottish kings as they made war on each other.

The priory owes its foundation to Sir Robert de Vaux, son of Sir Hubert de Vaux who was presented with the Barony of Gilsland by Henry II in the middle of the 12th century. Sir Robert settled on founding a house for the order of Augustinian canons and made a bequest generous enough to pay for the construction of the sizeable priory that we still see today.

By the turn of the 13th century most of the monastic buildings had been erected, together with the eastern part of the church. Work started on the nave a short time later and within twenty years the whole priory was finished.

Despite its size, it is unlikely that there was ever more than a small number of canons living at Lanercost, probably fewer than fifteen at any one time. Their lives would have been centred around the regular cycle of holy offices that lasted throughout the day, beginning with matins at midnight and running through until compline which was said before the canons went to bed. In a twenty-four day an average of one hour in every three would be spent in worship. The rest of their waking time was filled with a variety of work. In the north side of the cloister would have stood desks and chairs for writing and reading. There was the day-to-day business of running the priory and its estates to be attended to, and occasional visitors to be looked after.

For some 370 years this was the pattern of life at Lanercost, as it was at every other Augustinian house up and down the country. Close to the Scottish border the monastic tranquillity was broken from time to time by the arrival of friend and foe alike. In 1296 the Scots invaded the North and burned the cloister at Lanercost. A year later it again suffered at the hands of William Wallace. Edward I was a regular visitor, once stopping off in September 1306 with the intention of spending a few days. However, he fell ill during this short interlude and with winter coming on was obliged to stay until the following March! Accommodating the royal party of two hundred at rather short notice and for a period of six months must have placed a strain on the resources of the priory and, coupled with the local troubles that intruded throughout the time of the Border conflicts, it meant that from the middle of the 14th century onwards Lanercost had to struggle to survive.

This state of impoverishment brought about the priory's demise when Henry VIII instituted his Dissolution of the smaller monasteries in the country. The canons were expelled and the buildings passed to Sir Thomas Dacre, who rearranged the monks' accommodation to create a private house into which he moved in 1559.

The north aisle of the church was sealed off from the rest and became the parish church. A home was built for the vicar, and the other monastic buildings were allowed to fall into disrepair, many being plundered for their materials by local builders.

Nearly two centuries passed before it was decided to enlarge the parish church by restoring the nave. A new eastern wall was created by blocking the eastern arch and inserting three lights. A new roof was laid and the windows glazed, restoring the church to the condition in which we find it today.

Among the original buildings still standing is the gatehouse, which served as the porter's lodge in the time of the canons. Similarly the eastern end of the vicarage incorporates the guest-house where royal visitors like Edward I and Robert Bruce and other distinguished guests would have stayed.

The west front shows the Early English style at its best. Near the apex is a figure of St Mary Magdalene flanked by two coats of arms, that on the left belonging to Sir Thomas Dacre of Naworth Castle, father of the Sir Thomas Dacre who moved to Lanercost after the departure of the canons. His tomb stands in the ruined part of the church, though the brass fillet bearing his memorial inscription is now situated close to the organ.

The south wall of the nave contains two doors, now blocked, which led into the cloister and through one of which the canons would progress every Sunday morning after high mass, to walk right round the cloister before returning to the high altar through the second door.

As with so much of the building work at Lanercost, many of the stones in the cloister came from the old Roman wall and several carry inscriptions. There are also a number of Roman altars brought from neighbouring settlements associated with the wall which are now housed in the *cellarium* below what was the refectory, where the canons took their meals. The refectory has disappeared from the south side of the cloister, but the cellarium, where food was stored, is still in a good state of repair.

The dormitory where the canons slept would have been the upper storey of the long building that was built along the eastern side of the cloister. On the western side stood a range of store-rooms and offices, maybe too the library.

There are a number of interesting tombs in the ruined part of the church. Several members of the Howard family lie buried in the north transept, and on the north wall is the tomb of Sir Robert de Vaux's nephew, Sir Rowland de Vaux, which is the oldest in the church.

Ruined as the transepts, tower and roofless choir may be, they still retain a soaring majesty that recalls the great days of Lanercost Priory and, by extension, those of the nine hundred or so monastic houses spread throughout England during the Middle Ages.

St Peter and St Paul, Lavenham, Suffolk

6 MILES NORTH-EAST OF SUDBURY ON A1141

The Suffolk town of Lavenham preserves in its timber-framed houses, superb guildhall and splendid church the spirit of prosperity that grew out of the medieval wool trade.

The building of the present church stemmed from the suggestion made in 1485 by John de Vere, thirteenth earl of Oxford and lord of the manor, that the people of Lavenham might care to erect a brand-new church to celebrate Henry Tudor's defeat of Richard III at the Battle of Bosworth earlier in the year. The people of Lavenham agreed with the scheme, and several wealthy merchants donated considerable sums of money for the work. Among them were the Spryng family, notably 'The Rich Clothier' as he became known, Thomas Spryng, who gave 300 marks towards the building of the tower. Rising 141 feet and built of Barbeck stone with buttresses with flush flintwork walls, the simple, massive tower displays the merchant marks of the Spryngs as well as their coat of arms which appears thirty-two times around the parapet. The arms of de Vere which appear on the plinth show that the Earl of Oxford also played a substantial part in the erection of the tower, the first part of the church to be built.

However, de Vere's particular contribution was the

165

superbly carved and fan-vaulted south porch through which the church is entered.

To the left of the south door stands the 14th-century Purbeck marble font, mutilated, though older than the walls and pillars that surround it. For several years there was no nave to the church, the original one having been demolished when building work began on the tower. When the masons and carpenters did turn their attention to it they constructed a nave of great spaciousness with a well-proportioned *clerestory*. Although light and bright today, the windows would originally have been filled with stained glass.

In the north aisle stands the intricately carved Spryng *parclose* within which 'The Rich Clothier' was buried with his second wife, Alice. The Spryng coat of arms appears many times, along with Sts Catherine and Blaise. Delicate fan-vaulting springs from the top of the arches above which rises equally delicate tracery. The parclose was probably the work of Flemish craftsmen, and ranks among the best of early 16th-century work in English parish churches.

The chancel screen, adorned with foliage and flowers and the heads of animals and humans, is an equally fine piece of carving from the middle of the 14th century. This stands not only as a physical dividing point between the nave and chancel, but as an aesthetic separation of the two distinct styles in which they were built, for the 'post-Bosworth' nave was added to the chancel of the original church, which had been built in the Decorated style of the first half of the 14th century.

The chancel has a more intimate feel than the nave. There is more wood here, too: well-worked choir-stalls with an interesting collection of *misericords*. The *reredos* and east window are both Victorian, donations of the then incumbent, the Reverend Joseph Croker.

Another of Thomas Spryng's gifts to the church was

the Lady chapel, whose windows are now filled with early 19th-century painted glass showing a number of episodes from Christ's life and ministry, and from those of St Paul and St Stephen (the first martyr). The outside of the chapel bears the inscription 'Pray for the souls of Thomas Spryng Esq., and of Alice his wife, who caused this chapel to be built in the year of our Lord, 1525.'

In addition to its stately presence on top of the hill overlooking the town, the tower of Lavenham church also possesses a celebrated peal of bells which achieved national fame when they were broadcast ringing out the news of the death of Queen Mary. The tenor bell, weighing over a ton, is particularly famous. Cast in 1625 by Miles Graye of Colchester it has been called 'the finest toned bell in England, probably in the world'.

St Mary, Lastingham, North Yorkshire

Lastingham lies nestled in a dip of the ridge that divides Farndale from Rosedale. Thirteen hundred years ago this was a wild, inhospitable tract of moorland, far from any habitation.

However, it was this very barrenness that attracted St Cedd to Lastingham in the middle of the 7th century, after the Northumbrian King Ethelwald had invited him to found a monastery. Cedd wanted his new house of God to thrive and prosper in a wilderness; and prosper it did, for Lastingham has been a site of Christian worship ever since.

Bede, writing at Jarrow almost a century later, records the founding of St Cedd's monastery in some detail and also notes the manner of its founder's death; Cedd died at Lastingham during a period of plague and was buried there. As Bede records, a stone church dedicated to the Virgin Mary was later constructed and the saint's body was reinterred next to the altar. St Chad, St Cedd's brother (there were two other brothers in the family who were also priests), took charge of the abbacy of the monastery and later became Bishop of York and then of Lichfield.

The Danish invasion during the 9th and 10th centuries destroyed the stone church described by Bede and any

168

history of the monastery that it served. It wasn't until 1078 that Lastingham reappeared on the ecclesiastical map when St Stephen, Abbot of Whitby, asked permission of William the Conqueror to restore St Cedd's monastery. The surroundings had improved little in the intervening centuries and Abbot Stephen's stay was short-lived. Nevertheless the work he started marked the foundations of the church of St Mary as it stands today.

The first building undertaken by the abbot's workmen was the building of a crypt on the site of the Saxon church, to act as a shrine to St Cedd. This simple structure, virtually unchanged since Norman times, is a church in itself with aisles and an *apse*, making it unique among English crypts. An entrance was made on the north side, allowing pilgrims direct access from the outside to pray at St Cedd's grave.

In the crypt are also preserved stones, richly decorated, that belonged to earlier structures. There is a 9th-century crosshead which it is estimated came from a churchyard cross that would have stood some twenty-four feet high, one of the largest pre-Norman monuments in the country. Other stones show evidence of occupation after the Danish invasion, including a roughly hewn Danish 'hogback' tombstone which shows a bear with a bar across its mouth.

The abbey church as planned by Abbot Stephen would have been a far larger building than St Mary's is now. The present west end would have been the east end of the original church, with the main part stretching westwards into what is now the churchyard. The two massive pillars and the two now incorporated into the west wall would have been the base of a central tower. But Abbot Stephen's plans were never realized. He left Lastingham and moved to York, where he built St Mary's Abbey, with priests from York serving the community at Lastingham. Only in 1230 was St Mary's at Lastingham converted to a parish church, the building work having been completed two years earlier by blocking off the west end and building out the side aisles. A century later the south aisle was extended and the bell tower added.

The church also houses a copy of John Jackson's painting *Agony in the Garden*. Jackson was a native of Lastingham who undertook the restoration of St Mary's in 1828. At that time his painting was hung above the main altar, forming the focal point of the church. Today it hangs over the altar in the Lady chapel.

The Calvary on the south side of the church has an interesting history, having been captured from the Spanish man-of-war *Salvador del Mundo* at the battle of Cape St Vincent in 1797. It found its way to Lastingham via an antique shop in York and a generous local benefactor.

Holy Trinity, Long Melford, Suffolk

Long Melford is aptly named. Its main street is said to be three miles long, and, until the bridge was built in 1792, there was a ford here as well. Viewed from a distance across the attractive green Holy Trinity stands proudly above the village, almost cathedral-like in its proportions with eighteen *clerestory* windows set above twelve main windows on each side admirably achieving the 'glasshouse' effect sought by craftsmen of the Perpendicular period. The Lady chapel, almost a separate building standing at the east end of the church, is unusual too. Common features as they were of cathedrals or abbey churches, Long Melford is almost the only parish church never to have been an abbey that has one so situated.

Like Lavenham, Long Melford is a cloth church built from wealth acquired from the medieval wool trade, notably by the Clopton family. The church was completed in the year 1484. However, the list of rectors, which goes back as far as the end of the 12th century, and the confirmed presence of a church as early as 1050, indicates that the site is a long-established place of worship. There has even been the suggestion that there may have been a Roman temple here in ancient times. Not that that would have cut much ice with the clothiers of the Middle Ages, who confidently disposed of most of the previous structure in order to build their own splendid church. Only the five bays at the west end of the nave, and perhaps the

171

porch, remain from the old church built about a century earlier. Apart from these, the only exception to the late 15th-century construction is the tower which was built in 1903 as Long Melford's tribute to Queen Victoria's Diamond Jubilee.

There is some fine medieval glass in the windows of the north aisle showing members of the Clopton family, as might be expected; John Clopton, the principal benefactor of Holy Trinity, appears in the central upper part of the third window from the right. It's said that John Tenniel, who illustrated Lewis Carroll's *Alice in Wonderland*, modelled his Duchess on the image of Elizabeth, Duchess of Norfolk, which appears at the bottom of the window second from the left.

At the east end of the north aisle stands the Clopton *chantry* chapel with its magnificent roof, the frieze of which carries on painted scrolls two poems by the so-called Monk of Bury [St Edmunds], John Lydgate. Lydgate was a prodigious poet who composed an estimated 130,000 lines of verse in his time and served for a while in the early 15th century as the court poet. The 'Lily Crucifix' window in this chapel has also attracted considerable attention, showing as it does the traditional flower associated with the Virgin Mary presented in the form of the cross on which her son is shown suffering and dying.

The tomb of John Clopton stands in the chancel to the left of the high altar where it once acted as an Easter sepulchre (described earlier in Hawton church on page 133). Above the altar is a *reredos* carved from Caen stone in 1877 and based on Albrecht Dürer's painting of the Crucifixion. Opposite John Clopton's tomb is that of Sir William Cordell, Speaker of the House of Commons under Mary Tudor, and Master of the Rolls under her step-sister Elizabeth I. Sir William built both Melford Hall and the hospital named after him in the village. His tomb is regarded as one of the best examples of the work of Cornelius Cure, Master Mason to the Crown, who counted among his other memorials those in Westminster Abbey to Elizabeth I and Mary, Queen of Scots.

Behind the high altar lies the priest's vestry and behind that the virtually independent Lady chapel built in 1496. Around the central area runs an indoor cloister of sorts, lending a feeling of intimacy. Behind the altar hang curtains from part of the material woven and hung in Westminster Abbey for the Queen's coronation in 1953; it carries a gold crown and design of rose, thistle, leek and shamrock on a blue background.

There's a curious Chinese-style clock here, dating from the 18th century, and on the east wall a multiplication table from around the same time, reminding the visitor that from 1670 until the early 1800s the chapel served as the village school, a tradition that is maintained in some degree by the Sunday School which meets here during morning service.

St James, Louth, Lincolnshire

26 MILES NORTH-EAST OF LINCOLN, ON A157

St James's, Louth, has been described by Mervyn Blatch as 'one of the unforgettable churches of England, not only for its wonderful tower and spire but also for its spacious and beautifully proportioned interior'. He echoes other authorities of church architecture like Francis Bond, who referred to the church's crowning glory as 'that queen of English spires' designed by 'a genius among masons', and Alec Clifton-Taylor who summarized the admiration generally expressed for this Gothic masterpiece when he wrote, 'This is both the loftiest (about 295 feet) and the last (1501–1515) of our medieval parish church spires, and a most noble design'.

Noble it indeed is, standing proudly above the town, a distinctive landmark for miles around. The tower and spire are almost equal in height and ideally matched. Delicate flying buttresses add graceful support to the spire, springing from pinnacles that themselves reach a height of over fifty feet. Impressive by day, the tower and *crocketed* spire soar majestically into the darkness when floodlit at night.

The rebuilding of the church in the Perpendicular style was completed in 1474, but work didn't stop there. In the final year of the 15th century fresh work began on the spire, first the strengthening of the tower roof, followed two years later by the beginning of building work on the spire proper. This lasted until 1515 during which

174

time, according to the churchwardens' record, the whole community pulled together to achieve their common aim. 'For fifteen years', runs the account in *The First Churchwarden's Book of Louth*, 'with scanty labour and scantier means, the work was carried on. They borrowed from the guilds and the richer inhabitants, they pledged their silver crosses and chalices. From the richest to the poorest all seem to have been affected by a like zeal.' When the work was completed and the spire topped off with the weathercock made from a great copper basin captured from the Scots at the Battle of Flodden Field in 1513, there was free bread and ale, bell-ringing and a 'Te Deum' to greet the consecration of the new spire which had cost the grand sum of £305 8s. 5d!

Twenty-one years later this same civic pride in St James's sparked off the Lincolnshire Rising which led to the Pilgrimage of Grace in which the men of the North rose in armed defence of the monasteries threatened by Henry VIII. A sermon preached in the church on 1 October 1536, responding to rumours predicting the confiscation of church property (which in Louth included both St James's and the fine Cistercian abbey) led to widespread unrest. This was quickly stifled by the king, who referred gruffly to the townspeople and those of the surrounding area as the 'rude commons of one shire, and that, one of the most brutal and beestlie of the whole realm'. Then came the Pilgrimage of Grace itself, which was brought to a brutal end the following year when among those hanged at Tyburn were the Vicar of Louth and at least sixty other men from the town. But the end of their protests also marked the end of the abbey at Louth, of which only a few shattered fragments and a series of mounds remain.

The church was considerably restored in the last century by James Fowler, to whom its present appearance is due. The splendid Georgian ceiling has recently been cleaned and restored to its original appearance, with the plaster angels and bosses painted once again in Georgian colours. There are 19th-century corporation pews at the front of the nave, carved by Thomas Wilkinson Wallis of Louth, who decorated them with animals and birds. Wallis also carved the pulpit with its eleven disciples and the head of Judas Iscariot looking out from the stone foliage in the base, and the choir-stalls where he recorded the church's gratitude to Fowler for his restoration work by carving his head near the organ.

Two oak angels carved for the original nave roof are mounted either side of the altar in the Angel chapel, facing six medieval stalls with *misericords*. In the corresponding area on the south side of the nave is St Stephen's chapel with its medieval *sedilia* and war memorials to those from Louth who died at home as well as abroad in the two World Wars.

At the other end of the church stands the lofty west arch, framing the great west window presented to St James's in 1874 by Cornelius Parker, who is shown in the window wearing a red cap. Below him, wearing a red cassock, is Canon Wilde, incumbent of Louth for over fifty years from 1859 to 1914.

Returning finally to the magnificent tower, seen this time from the inside, the glorious vaulted ceiling with the sunburst at the centre hangs eighty-six feet above the floor. The sunburst was the emblem of Edward IV, in whose reign the tower was built, and here it disguises the circular trap-door into the ringing chamber through which the bells would have been hoisted to ring out the first celebration of the building of this glorious church five hundred years ago.

St Wendreda, March, Cambridgeshire

St Wendreda is very much a saint of the eastern counties. Her father, King Anna, was a 7th-century ruler of the East Saxons and Wendreda was brought up in his royal palace at Exning near Newmarket. However, the princess preferred a quieter life than that of the court and gave up whatever fun and games the 7th-century palace had to offer in order to devote herself to healing both humans and animals. Her love of solitude makes the chaotic progress of her relics around the country throughout the Middle Ages all the more poignant.

Interred first at March, where she had spent her declining years, the saint was first uprooted to be transferred to Ely. She spent only a brief spell there before being dug up again to be carried at the head of the Saxon army as it marched against the Danes in 1016. Unfortunately, St Wendreda's presence did not achieve the victory the Saxons hoped for and her relics fell into the hands of the Danes and their king, Canute. He is said to have been so moved by the story of her selfless piety that he turned to Christianity and later presented her relics to the church at Canterbury. There she stayed for the next three hundred years until 1343 when she was on the move again, back to March this time, to be enshrined in the newly refurbished church dedicated to her.

177

The church in which the saint was laid to rest was probably the third on the site. Although no evidence remains of its existence, it seems likely that there was a simple Saxon church in March, possibly during the saint's lifetime. Then there is the font, the only surviving remnant of the second church, which shows that a Norman church was almost certainly built here, standing on the area now occupied by the nave.

The tower was built in the second half of the 14th century, a decade or two after the church had been almost completely rebuilt to accommodate the returning St Wendreda after her wanderings.

Her return was soon followed by the arrival of pilgrims eager to visit her shrine in search of a cure. They in turn brought further prosperity to the town, which found its fullest and most glorious expression in the church's breathtaking double hammer-beam angel roof, which many experts hold to be the finest in the country, and even, according to some, in Europe.

There are 118 angels in all, several of them half life-size, which project from the hammer-beams and other principal roof timbers, all carved from English oak. Between the hammer-beams are more angels in half-relief. There are also figures of the Apostles, martyrs and saints standing beneath canopies on the wall posts, beneath whom are yet more angels carrying medieval musical instruments. The saints are identified by their various emblems of martyrdom, or the like: St Lawrence with his gridiron, St Andrew with the cross named after him, St Stephen with stones in his hands, St Peter with his key, to name four of the twenty. Among the musical instruments you can see a set of bagpipes, a harp, a shawm and a lute. Even the devil is tucked away up there, too, not that he is easy to find; though looking carefully for him is one way of looking closely at, and therefore fully appreciating, the extraordinary feat of engineering as well as of creative mastery that went into this roof.

The roof at March was built during the fifty years that span the turn of the 16th century, and marks the high point in church roof construction. Nothing so glorious was ever created again in a parish church, partly because of the Reformation, but also because the double hammer-beam is not actually the most robust of structures, which explains why the carpenters at March wisely added iron rods to brace their masterpiece against the combined pressures of gravity and outward thrust that threaten such a high-pitched structure.

The 'belt and braces' approach was not in vain. Neither death-watch beetle nor reforming zealots have managed to bring serious damage to the heavenly ensemble that look down from the roof of St Wendreda's as they have done for the best part of five centuries.

All Saints, Martock, Somerset

Many of the buildings in Martock are built of Ham stone from the famous Ham Hill quarries a few miles away to the north-west, and foremost among these is the church of All Saints. Perpendicular in style, this has one of the grandest interiors found in the whole county – thanks to the glorious and lavishly decorated tie-beam roof which is set off to perfection against the golden stone.

This is a remarkable piece of carpentry. Panels of various pierced designs lie between the rafters and secondary purlins. The huge tie-beams themselves are decorated with four-petal flowers and carry delicate crestings. There are angels at the centre of each with outstretched wings and carrying shields. Above them is more pierced tracery in the form of *quatrefoils*, and to complete the elaborate ensemble carved pendants hang down in intricate and ornate detail.

At one time the *clerestory* was filled with stained glass depicting a total of 120 coats of arms, not a shard of which remains. However, the canopied niches between the windows have survived, preserving their delicate carvings – no two of which are the same. The figures of the twelve Apostles painted on the backs of the niches appeared in the 17th century and though there may not have been statues in the niches originally, the present figures are interesting examples of contemporary fashion.

Both from the outside and the inside, St Edmund, Southwold (above), gives an impression of peaceful harmony and space while Holy Trinity, Long Melford (below) is almost cathedral-like in its proportions.

St Mary, West Walton (above), marks a highlight in medieval church architecture and St Peter and St Paul, Salle (below), ranks as one of the country's most magnificent village churches.

The nave displays the medieval prosperity of Martock, which thrived on the cloth trade during the Middle Ages. Elegant piers support well-proportioned arches. There are angel *corbels* bearing shields, some plain, others charged with devices like the Tudor rose or the arms of the de Widcombe family (which also appear on the parapet outside).

The chancel, in comparison, is simple and unadorned, contrasting the wealth of the congregation with the more modest means that the rector, whose property the chancel was, had to draw on. At one time it was separated from the nave by what a late 18th-century commentator described as a 'superb open-work Gothic screen of fourteen arches, supporting an enriched cornice of excellent carving in fine preservation. Over the screen is a *rood-loft* thirty feet long and seventeen feet wide'. Sad to say, nothing remains of this except for a short length on the sill of the east window to remind us of its former glory.

Outside the church there's an interesting reminder of a popular pastime from several centuries ago. At one time the lower stage of the tower and its buttresses formed a makeshift fives court (the game was apparently widely played in the area). In order to retrieve balls hit on to the roof of the aisle, notches were cut into the buttress to provide footholds and handholds. Windows were broken sometimes, too, and when a piece of masonry was accidentally knocked off and landed on a bystander's head, the churchwardens moved in and stopped people playing fives around the church altogether. The cemented-up notches and the worn state of the buttresses are silent reminders of the vigorous and energetic activity that was once focused on them.

St Michael and St Mary, Melbourne, Derbyshire

St Michael and St Mary's, Melbourne, is generally acknowledged to be one of the most ambitious Norman churches ever built in England. What it may lack in subtlety of detail it more than makes up for in massive simplicity and a uniformity of design that has remained almost unaltered for eight hundred years.

The church dates from the 12th century, and was begun in 1133, the year that the See of Carlisle was founded and the living at Melbourne was given to the bishop of that diocese. This was a troubled time for the northern regions and it seems likely that the bishop desired a place of retreat in times of conflict. Melbourne would have seemed an ideal location, which goes some way to explaining why a church of such awesome proportions should have been built in what must then have been a comparatively small village: if this was to be an episcopal church it needed to look like a cathedral in miniature. As a result Melbourne possesses features found in almost no other parish churches. There are three towers of sorts and a *clerestory* walk-way all round the nave.

Melbourne is also unusual in having a vestibule called a *narthex*. The stone vaulting may be crude (suggesting that this may have been the first part of the church to have been built), but the fact that there is a narthex at all implies the dignity that the architect sought to bestow on this church.

Close inside the nave stands the font, symbol of entry into the church through baptism. Beyond lies the nave, lined by its massive pillars fifteen feet high and four feet thick. These support solid Norman arches heavily decorated with the familiar zigzag design which in turn lead the eye up to the clerestory formed from triple-arch arcading, leading, on the north side at least, on to single round-headed windows. A clerestory with double pointed arches opening to twin pointed windows replaced the Norman one on the south side in the 13th century, although the survival of the Norman arcading at the eastern end of the south clerestory indicates that this pattern must have originally surrounded the whole nave.

It is interesting to see as well that the *rood* has been restored to its rightful place above the eastern end of the nave.

At the entrance to the sanctuary the pillars are topped by capitals displaying a wealth of foliage interwoven with curious grotesques. There is a squint at the base of the pillar on the north corner beside the Lady chapel, through which it is possible to see the cross on the high altar. These occur in many medieval churches and may have been incorporated as a means of letting the priests celebrating at the side altars follow the priest at the high altar, since several masses would be in progress at the same time.

When the church was first built the nave would have had an even more impressive appearance by virtue of the three semicircular *apses* built at its eastern end. These presumably deteriorated more rapidly than the rest of the building, for in the 17th century it became necessary to pull them down to be crudely replaced by square ends to the chancel and transepts.

Further large-scale restoration was undertaken by Sir Gilbert Scott in 1862.

St Mary the Virgin, Melton Mowbray, Leicestershire

Melton Mowbray merits its distinction as the stateliest church in Leicestershire for a number of reasons. Its dimensions alone are impressive, 154 feet long with a grand central tower 100 feet high, unfortunately spoilt on its north side by an external stair turret which mars its otherwise regular features. The Perpendicular *clerestory* which contains no fewer than forty-eight windows (twenty-four in the nave and twelve in each transept) is striking. Inside, the transepts each have north and south aisles, features denied many cathedrals and found in only three other parish churches in the country, of which Patrington (described on pages 198–200) is one.

St Mary's was largely built in the half century between 1280 and 1330 and includes examples of Early English, Decorated and Perpendicular work. The oldest part of the church is the lower part of the tower and the staircase, which are about a century earlier, dating from around 1170. The bell-ringing chamber in this section of the tower is more reminiscent of a fortress than a church, with huge walls measuring over four feet in thickness and narrow, deeply recessed windows with sloping jambs and sills.

During the next fifty years the lovely Early English pointed arches were introduced, along with the clusters of round pillars. The tower was heightened at the same time and a spire was added.

Come 1330 the Decorated church was more or less complete and remained so for a century and a half until the last major changes came about. These did away with the spire and heightened the tower in its place. The magnificent clerestory was built containing more than fifteen thousand pieces of glass in its forty-eight windows. And the whole church was topped with a continuous series of battlements, with a matching set for the tower. Finally, a vestry was added to the north side of the chancel. Dated 1532, that marked the last significant construction in the church.

The best view of the church can be gained from the western end, where the Galilee porch affords an ideal sight-line through the nave and aisles, the two double-aisled transepts, the tower crossing and into the chancel. The Galilee porch has had a somewhat chequered history, reaching its low point in the eighteenth century when it served for a time as the 'garage' for the town fire engine! (The John Milton whose tombstone lies in the floor of the porch is not the author of *Paradise Lost*; he was the tutor of the Duke of York, who later became King James II.)

In the corner next to the 19th-century font is a water pump encased in a carved wooden cupboard. If not unique in a parish church (or any church for that matter) it is certainly extremely unusual, though eminently useful.

The window above contains lovely old pieces of principally medieval stained glass, collected from different parts of the church and assembled here in 1820. Further along the south aisle is another window commemorating the three bishops, Latimer, Ridley and Cranmer, who were martyred in Oxford for adhering to their Protestant faith. Hugh Latimer was a Leicestershire man and preached a sermon, possibly his last, in St Mary's only a few days before he was arrested in 1553.

Below the martyrs' window lies the effigy of a crusader descended from the brother of the first Roger de Mowbray, lord of the manor. He is shown armed and with his legs crossed, possibly indicating that he had taken the crusader's vow. There are more interesting tombs in the Lady chapel in the eastern aisle of the south transept, where the almost life-size effigies of Edward and Katherine Pate lie side by side in Elizabethan clothes, with their eleven children, several of whom died as babies, gathered at their feet. Beside them lie Bartholomew Brooksby, a merchant of the Staple of Calais, and an alabaster lady garbed in the fashion of the late 14th century.

In the north transept sits the organ at which Sir Malcolm Sargent played when he was organist at St Mary's for ten years from 1914. Before the organ was installed this transept housed Melton School until the end of the 18th century.

No statues on the outside of the church survived the Reformation. The empty niches in the western porch are silent witnesses of their destruction. However, the ancient lead spouting along the nave clerestory did remain unscathed and shows a considerable amount of decoration. The monogram of the Virgin Mary appears on the heads of these spoutings, as well as the trefoil and the fleur-de-lis, both symbols of the cult of the Virgin that was popular in the late Middle Ages. In addition, the spout heads are all in the shape of a Marian crown.

St Mary, Nantwich, Cheshire

St Mary's, Nantwich, is by far the largest and grandest 14th century church in Cheshire. Cruciform in shape, it is topped by a distinctive octagonal tower, which is particularly appropriate since the town can be approached by eight different roads.

Like many churches in the county, St Mary's is built of a warm but crumbly local sandstone and the west end in particular was subject to extensive restoration work in the 19th century, not always to the building's benefit. Gilbert Scott masterminded this work and chose to replace the large Perpendicular west window with one filled with geometrical tracery. Beneath this he placed a doorway in the Early English style, claiming he had found evidence for its antecedent. His window certainly didn't go down terribly well with the people of Nantwich, and in 1875 they replaced it with the present one.

The nave of St Mary's dates from about 1320. The narrow western window in the north wall is probably the oldest in the church, though the glass, like most in the church, is Victorian. Since the church was built on a bed of sand saturated with water the nave arcades have been strengthened by internal flying buttresses thrown across the aisles. The piers have clustered shafts and the arches are deeply moulded.

At one time the windows contained a good deal of heraldic stained glass; this was gradually broken through civil unrest or general disregard during the 17th and 18th centuries. The pulpit suffered, too, from Gilbert Scott this time, who had the former three-decker pulpit cut down to make the present one at the same time as he removed the old box pews and galleries that once ran right round the nave and across the arch of the crossing.

With the galleries removed, the original line of the steeply sloping nave roof is clearly visible in the west wall of the crossing, indicating what the nave must have looked like before the roof was raised and the *clerestory* built to let in more light in the late 15th or early 16th century.

The four huge arches supporting the tower are even more elaborately moulded than those in the nave arcade. Those in the north and east are 13th century in style, while the south and west arches date from a century later. The stone pulpit is a rare and beautifully made Perpendicular one and the low screen wall probably acted as the base for a *rood screen* before that was demolished in the 16th century.

The north side of the crossing is one of the oldest parts of the church, dating from the 13th century; the Lady chapel in the north bay (now the vestry) was added later. There is some very old glass in the north window showing Jesse, the Virgin and Child, one of the three kings bearing frankincense, Christ's Nativity and the Archangel Michael. There are also two heads with foliage sprouting from their mouths in this window, a motif that is repeated in a stone head carved on the north-west pier and on the *poppy-head* on the desk before the south chancel choir stalls. These are all representations of the Green Man, the popular pagan tree or fertility god who is best remembered now for the number of pubs named after him.

The chancel is the great glory of St Mary's, built as the Decorated style was reaching its highest point of creative achievement. The side windows reflect the flowing curvilinear tracery that characterized Decorated work, while the east window and pierced battlements show the transition to the stiffer Perpendicular style.

Nantwich is unusual among parish churches in having a vaulted chancel, and certainly one as magnificent as the complex *lierne* vault built here. In all there are nearly seventy carved bosses. Those along the ridge display scenes from the life of Christ and the Virgin Mary; the others have a great variety of foliage.

To complement the roof there are twenty superb canopied choir-stalls which show close similarities with those in Chester Cathedral; they share a refinement of design and craftsmanship unsurpassed in medieval English wood-carving. Above the triple arches of each stall rise three canopied niches, the central one higher than those flanking it and each running down to the lower canopy heads.

Several of the subjects of the *misericords* are also repeated at Chester: the unicorn and virgin, the lion and dragon fighting and the fox pretending to be dead to snare birds. Other subjects include: a griffin eating a man, a mermaid, a wrestling match and a woman with a ladle beating a man with a spindle – all are as much vivid and beautifully worked examples of their creators' humour as their skill.

St Mary and St Barlok, Norbury, Derbyshire

Readers of George Eliot will be interested to discover that Norbury has connections with her novel, *Adam Bede*. Adam was based on her father Robert Evans, who was born in the parish in 1773, sang in the church choir and is said to have made the wooden altar that now stands in the north aisle. His parents lie buried in the churchyard at Norbury.

The church itself has close associations with the Fitzherbert family who were lords of the manor for over 750 years, from 1125 to 1881. Nicholas Fitzherbert, whose fine alabaster tomb now stands in the chancel, died in 1473 and according to an inscription originally mounted on the tomb is credited with much of the work on the present church. Apart from the chancel, most of what we see today dates from the 15th century. The wide spacious chancel dates from a century earlier. The roof was altered at the time of the construction of the nave, and the walls accordingly were heightened – as you can see, both inside and out.

Norbury's great treasure is its medieval glass, much of which still survives in the recently restored great east window and those of the north and south walls of the chancel. A century and half ago the great east window was the subject of a none too successful restoration which

190

took original glass from other parts of the church. This has been rectified in recent years and now the window displays the twelve Apostles, each bearing a scroll with part of the Apostle's Creed in Latin. Edward the Confessor is there, too, as is St Chad. Above the saints are nine heraldic circles in which appear a number of coats of arms, including those of the Fitzherberts.

The side windows of the chancel contain a display of colour and design, both heraldic and decorative, that is seldom found in the medieval glass of parish churches, and the centre intersection of the traceries of each window bears a distinctive twelve-petalled flower that is thought not to occur anywhere but at Norbury.

The chancel is further enhanced by the two very fine alabaster tombs that now stand on either side. Both date from the end of the 15th century and were probably commissioned by John Fitzherbert to commemorate his parents, Ralph and Elizabeth, and his grandfather, Nicholas. Nicholas is shown on the single tomb dressed in full armour with the figures of his two wives depicted in the panels at either end and the children they bore him in those along the sides. This tomb was first placed in the south-east chapel, where the windows still bear the arms of Nicholas Fitzherbert and his two wives.

The double tomb of Ralph and Elizabeth Fitzherbert was originally sited in the north-east chapel, where the organ now stands. Until 1842 a richly carved oak screen crossed the chancel and the first bay of the nave on each side, and the tomb stood inside this. But the tomb was moved to the chancel and the screen taken down. The figure of Elizabeth Fitzherbert provides a good example of the dress worn by women at the end of the 15th century.

The brass that lies between the two tombs commemorates Sir Anthony Fitzherbert, the youngest of Ralph's seven sons, who nevertheless eventually succeeded his elder brother John as the fourteenth lord of the manor of

Norbury in 1531. This brass is technically referred to as a *palimpsest*; that's to say it was originally put to a different use and has been recycled, so to speak. In this case the two portions probably came from memorial brasses in the convent at Croxden and the abbey at Calwich, both having been dissolved in the Reformation. Sir Anthony is shown in his robes as a judge in the Court of Common Pleas and beneath the figures is an epitaph in Latin that he is said to have composed.

In 1899 the north wall of the nave had to be rebuilt when signs of subsidence appeared, and this work revealed the two Saxon cross shafts that can now be seen in the church.

St Barlok, the Irish abbot and bishop to whom the church is dedicated, appears in the centre panel of the south window in the south-east chapel; his name is clearly readable. The cross-legged knight dressed in chain mail who lies under the arch dividing this chapel from the nave is Sir Henry Fitzherbert, the sixth lord of the manor. He is shown thrusting his sword back into his scabbard, an action that is interpreted as being the dying act of a faithful Christian who willingly gives up his soul to his Maker.

Of the principal features of Norbury church the oldest is its Early English font, dating from the beginning of the 13th century and most likely coming from the earlier church that stood on the site.

St Mary the Virgin, North Petherton, Somerset

Somerset has long been famous for its glorious church towers, of which North Petherton is one of the loveliest, a fact that makes the current need to raise funds to save it all the more pressing. Pevsner described it as 'a special "tour de force"' even among Somerset towers and, rising to a height of 108 feet above the village, it stands proudly in the centre of the community – a focal point for both the religious and secular comings and goings of North Petherton for the last five hundred years and, we must hope, for the next five hundred was well.

Elegantly proportioned and displaying just the right balance of ornamental enrichment, the tower has tall *crocketed* pinnacles adorning its top stage and smaller ones set diagonally on the stage below the parapet. Further elaborate decoration is found in the windows of the tower, all of which are filled with intricately pierced stone tracery which complements the handsome angled buttressing which dignifies the tower so impressively.

Built of locally quarried sandstone, the present Perpendicular church dates from the middle of the 15th century and is only the most recent in a succession of churches that most likely began back in the 9th century when Ina, King of the Saxons, was said to have settled in the parish.

It's possible that King Alfred dropped his famous jewel when he was returning from the little Saxon church at North Petherton. This was the enamelled head set in gold and bearing the inscription "Alfred had me made" that was found by a ploughman in 1693 and which now sits in the Ashmolean Museum in Oxford. A replica is on display in the church, in the *Piscina* on the east wall of the Portman chapel, and serves today as the insignia for the mayor of North Petherton.

Geoffrey Chaucer was probably another worshipper in the same church during his time as Warden of the forests of North Petherton. Chaucer had been dead for only some twenty years when the intricately carved pulpit was made, and building work on the new church was started not many years after that.

There is some fine carving to be seen in the early 17th-century bench ends, and the chancel screen completed in 1909 is admired as one of the best of its kind in the south-west.

Over the south door is a gallery, dating from 1623, decorated with elegant hammer-beams and further rich carving. Though probably built as a sort of church treasury, this may well have served as an armoury in later times.

Outside the north porch stands a large block of stone that formerly served as a market cross and from which mendicant friars once preached. The remains of decoration that can still be seen indicate that this, too, was once as elegantly decorated as the church.

St Mary the Virgin, Painswick, Gloucestershire

3 MILES NORTH-EAST OF STROUD, ON A46

Famous for its yew trees and table-top tombs, Painswick possesses England's finest churchyard which forms a fitting setting for the parish church of St Mary's in this prosperous little Cotswold town.

The wealth of Painswick, like so many parishes in the area, came from the wool industry and memorials to wool-traders of the 17th century can be found all round the church.

Painswick also owed its medieval prosperity in part to its famous quarries which supplied stone for many fine buildings in the neighbourhood, most notably the tower of Gloucester Cathedral.

In the 18th century this local stone came under the chisel of the Bryans, a Painswick family of carvers and masons whose work can be seen inside the church, but most notably in the churchyard, which for two centuries has been the village's focal point. At the same period the celebrated yew trees were planted, ninety-nine at any one time, but never it seems a round one hundred. Immaculately clipped and cared for, these form a perfect backdrop to the church's equally famous tombs.

Many of these must be the work of John Bryan, the elder son of the family, who designed and built the north-east gateway of which only the two outer pillars remain. His own tomb takes the impressive form of a plain stone pyramid bearing a memorial tablet to himself, his wife and daughter. Those of other prominent local families like the Packers, Pooles and Lovedays can be found grouped together around the large churchyard, displaying a rich variety of shapes and decoration from crowns and shells to cherubs and skeletons. There are two very helpful 'Tomb Trails' (available in the church porch) which guide the visitor round seventy-five of the best preserved and most interesting monuments.

The outside of St Mary's is also the setting for the delightful 'Clipping' ceremony that takes place on the afternoon of Sunday 19 September (or the first Sunday after that), which represents the Feast of the Nativity of the Blessed Virgin Mary, according to the old calendar. This has nothing whatsoever to do with the maintenance of the yews. The word 'clipping' may owe its etymology to the medieval word *yclept*, although the exact origin of the custom is unclear. In any event, one of the definitions given for 'clip' in the *Oxford English Dictionary*, 'To surround closely, encircle, encompass', aptly describes the ceremony in which clergy, choir and two or three hundred children join hands and encircle the church, moving backwards and forwards in the manner of a country dance while a special hymn is sung. After the ceremony the children are rewarded with a traditional Painswick bun and a silver coin.

St Mary's is also justly proud of its fine peal of bells, among the best in the country. The ringers, known engagingly as the Ancient Society of Painswick Youths, have been ringing the changes since 1686 and the peal book contains details of many famous peals lasting upwards of eight hours.

The tower bears the marks of history from slightly earlier in the 17th century, when it was struck by

St Mary, Stow, showing the remarkable font decorated with non-Christian symbols.

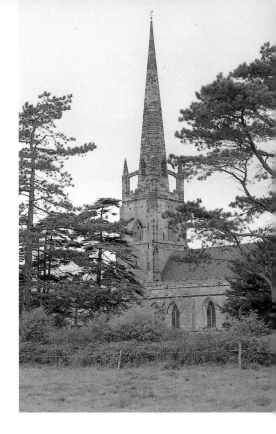

Both St Mary, Ashwell (above left) and St Andrew, Clifton Campville (above right), are renowned for their distinctive spires while St Mary, Astbury (below), glories in its fifteenth-century roofs.

St Mary the Virgin, Melton Mowbray (above left), is known for its impressive stately dimensions and St Michael and St Mary, Melbourne (above right) for its simple uniformity of design. Below, St Peter, Wootton Wawen, has grown over the centuries around a Saxon tower.

The intricately carved Easter Sepulchre in All Saints, Hawton, is a remarkable feature of the church.

cannon-balls fired during the Civil War. Charles I stayed in Painswick in 1643 after a defeat his forces inflicted on those of Parliament and one of the pillars in the nave bears an inscription supposedly scratched by a Parliamentarian soldier held prisoner in the church in 1644. 'Be bolde, be bolde, but not too bold,' he cautioned.

St Patrick, Patrington, Humberside

St Patrick's, Patrington, plays 'Queen of Holderness' to Hedon's 'King' (described on pages 138–40) and is an incomparable parish church that richly deserves its acclaim. The church is widely regarded as a masterpiece of the Decorated style and earned from Alec Clifton-Taylor the glowing testimony of being 'one of the great parish churches of England, one which would be certain of a place on any expert's list of the dozen finest'.

Without doubt its immense appeal lies in its uniformity of design and construction. With the Archbishops of York as patrons, St Patrick's never suffered from the shortage of funds that prolonged the building programmes of other churches. There is none of the cheerful conglomeration of styles and in some cases materials that lend charm and character to so many country churches. Patrington offers a purity of conception and construction which from start to finish lasted just over a century. As a result there is harmony throughout. Nothing jars. Nothing seems out of place. Even the modern additions blend pleasingly with the medieval work, which at Patrington reaches one of the highest levels of attainment in the north of England; the association with Robert de Patrington who became master mason at York Minster in the latter part of the 14th century seems to confirm the availability of a high degree of local craftsmanship at the time the church was built.

Little remains of previous churches on the site. There was more than likely a Saxon church, which was equally likely to have been destroyed by Danes raiding up the Humber. Stones used in the present church bear witness to a Norman predecessor and the first pier in the north-western part of the nave stands on a large 13th-century base, which shows that a sizeable church was at least started here before the present one, even if it may never have been completed.

St Patrick's is cruciform in plan, with double aisles to the nave and both transepts (the latter is a rare feature that it shares with Melton Mowbray, as described on page 184). As a result of this design the whole of the weight of the tower and spire rest on the four large central piers. Rising to 189 feet to the top of the weathercock, the spire is completely plain and reaches upwards to the sky through, in Alec Clifton-Taylor's words, 'a rich Gothic diadem . . . an original conception of considerable charm'.

Inside the church the skill of the masons becomes apparent both in the quality and beauty of the arcades as well as in the profusion of carved faces on the capitals of the pillars and the intricacy of the foliage carved on others.

In spite of the comparatively short time in which the church was built, it spanned the ravages of the Black Death which put an effective stop to all building in the middle of the 14th century. In consequence the transepts, which were built first, have window tracery that is noticeably geometric in design. Next came the nave, by which time the windows had developed curvilinear tracery. Then came the Black Death, to be followed by a new generation of masons who set about work on the chancel and more or less copied the nave windows in building the side windows of this part of the church. When they got to the east window, however, they built it with the Perpendicular tracery of their own age.

At one time the south transept was occupied by three chapels, of which the *piscinas* and the altar of the Lady Chapel remain. There were three chapels in the north transept, too, and one has recently been re-established in honour of the Holy Cross of Jesus, a dedication enhanced by the oil painting that once hung over the high altar. From the south transept you can see the unusual staircase that leads to the ringing chamber in the tower over the crossing. This climbs over the south arch of the crossing, looking rather like a stepped gable and no more reassuring for anyone with a bad head for heights. Between the Commonwealth period and the last century (when it was returned to its former position) the twelve-panelled stone font stood in the crossing beneath the ringing chamber.

The chancel lies through a screen constructed mainly of old wood, with a venerable lock attached to the door. Ahead stands the high altar backed by the *reredos* designed by Harold Gibbons, which was installed in 1936 in memory of George V, who was lord of the manor. In the centre stand the Blessed Virgin and Holy Child flanked by twelve Northumbrian saints, and the larger figures of St Patrick himself and St George.

In the sanctuary Patrington also has a fine Easter sepulchre similar to those at Hawton in Nottinghamshire and Heckington in Lincolnshire (both of which have been mentioned already). Here the upper section is now blank, though it probably contained a depiction of the Ascension, or the Coronation of the Virgin Mary. The *sedilia* and *piscina* on the other side have beautiful carved canopies that complement the elaborate decoration found in other parts of the church.

St Nicholas, Pyrford, Surrey

St Nicholas, Pyrford, is one of the oldest churches in Surrey that remains as a complete building from a single period. Built in about the middle of the 12th century of a dark flinty conglomerate known as 'pudding-stone', with massive walls three feet thick in places, it has stayed structurally almost unchanged for eight hundred years.

Writing in the last century Sir Thomas Jackson, who restored part of the interior in 1869, observed, 'Humble and modest as the building is, it has always seemed to me the very model of a small English church. Nothing could be happier than the site that has been chosen for it, on the brow of a steep bank overlooking the broad meadows through which the Wey winds, with Newark Priory in the middle distance and the chalk hills beyond. Nothing can be more perfectly artistic than the way in which the building is adapted to its site from every point of view. It is to these elements of design that the church owes its charm. Of positive architectural ornament it is almost bare, and none could be added without spoiling it.'

The site has a particular interest for, situated as it is in its circular churchyard on an isolated bluff above the river, St Nicholas may stand on a pre-Christian place of worship associated with the Pyrford Stone, an ancient monument at the top of the hill beyond the church.

Like many Norman churches, St Nicholas was built without foundations and so heavy were the walls that

201

the need for buttressing must have arisen soon after the church had been built. The three original buttresses were built of Sarsen stone, the others were added during the 19th century.

Pyrford is also distinguished in retaining three of its twelve consecration crosses, incised in the north and south walls of the chancel and west wall of the nave at the time the church was consecrated by the Norman bishop eight centuries ago.

Traces of wall paintings have been found showing (on the south wall) a scene depicting the flagellation of Christ and a primitive representation of the struggle between good and evil in which appears a row of men wearing conical hats. They are unlike any others found in wall paintings, although they have similarities to sculptures of soldiers at Barfreston in Kent and Kilpeck in Herefordshire (both described earlier).

A certain amount of restoration took place in the 15th century, when new windows were created in the nave and pews were fitted. The roofs of both chancel and nave were probably refitted at this time, and the lovely north porch built.

Although the *rood* was no doubt broken up during the Reformation, Jackson recalls the appearance of the *celure* (canopy over the rood) at the east end of the nave. Constructed of feather-edged, grooved boarding, it was apparently painted with 'yellow flowers and rosettes on a red ground'.

In another act of his restoration Jackson removed a thick layer of white paint from the Jacobean pulpit to reveal an interesting combination of woods: red deal, oak and walnut or cedar. Dated 1628, this may have been a gift of Nicholas Burley, who lived in the Old House at Pyrford in the early part of the 17th century.

St Mary and Ethelflaeda, Romsey, Hampshire

Romsey Abbey dates back to the beginning of the 10th century when King Edward the Elder, son of Alfred the Great, founded a nunnery at Romsey and a simple Saxon church was built to serve the community. This probably lasted no later than the end of the century, when Danish raids laid waste much of the south coast of England.

A new church was built at the beginning of the 11th century and two carved stone *roods* (two of the abbey's greatest treasures) date from this period.

It is the Norman rebuilding work of the 12th century that forms the greater part of the church today. Massive and uncompromising externally, with a squat central tower topped by a wooden bell cage, it contains inside some of the most perfect Norman work seen anywhere in England. The western end of the nave was built in the early English style towards the middle of the 12th century, and the nave aisles were added in the 15th century to provide greater accommodation for the parishioners, but the fabric of the church remains largely unaltered since Henry de Blois, Bishop of Winchester, undertook his building programme beginning with the choir and transepts around the year 1120.

On the southern side of the church, beside the Abbess's ornately carved doorway with its elaborate arch and pillars, stands one of the abbey's two Saxon roods. Beneath a modern canopy that keeps off the worst of the weather, the hand of God is depicted pointing down from a cloud to his Son. Christ is shown standing erect on the cross with his arms spread wide not in suffering but in welcome.

Inside, the church presents some of the grandest and most detailed Norman work seen anywhere. The nave is over 250 feet long and soars to a height of seventy feet on tall columns that support the *triforium*, unique tm'zo Romsey, in which each bay contains twin sub-arches with a little pillar in the space above.

Throughout the church there are interesting and important memorials. At the western end lies Sir William Petty, a native of Romsey and founder member of the Royal Society who counted Pepys and John Evelyn among his friends, and who is commemorated in a fine Victorian monument erected by one of his descendants. In the St Nicholas chapel of the south transept Earl Mountbatten of Burma is commemorated by a simple floor tablet; he lived nearby at Broadlands. On the wall above him is the memorial to John and Grisel St Barbe, former owners of Broadlands, which Lord Louis restored. On the south wall is a superb Gothic canopied tomb in which lies the Purbeck marble effigy of an unidentified 13th-century lady.

When the abbey was first built, both north and south transepts had *apsed* chapels on their eastern sides. These have now been separated off to act as vestries, and opposite the door to the south vestry is a glass case containing several of Romsey's treasures, including the deed of sale signed by Henry VIII which enabled the parishioners to buy the abbey for £100 after the suppression of the nunnery.

In the apsed chapel of St Anne at the end of the south choir aisle the abbey's other Saxon rood stands above the altar. This low-relief carving of the Crucifixion may well be the oldest in England and could be the crucifix recorded as a gift made by King Edgar to Romsey Abbey at about the year 960. Christ is shown on the cross with two angels above and the haloed figures of his mother and St John standing below. Two Roman soldiers stand below them, one with a spear, the other holding aloft a sponge of vinegar. However, branches are seen shooting from the cross as vivid symbols of the triumph of life over death.

At the eastern end of the church are two small chapels in what is known as the retrochoir, which were built as doorways into the now demolished Lady chapel at the eastern end of the church. In St Ethelflaeda's chapel there is the coffin lid of a former abbess, whose carved hand is shown emerging from her tomb to grasp her staff of office. Next door is St Mary's chapel, which has part of a 13th-century wall painting thought to show scenes from the life of St Nicholas.

Perhaps the abbey's most spectacular painting is the 16th-century wooden painted *reredos* in the north transept (known as St Lawrence's chapel, since the area formed the chancel of the parish church of St Lawrence which served the congregation before the Reformation). This reredos once stood behind the high altar and shows in its upper row nine assorted saints and unnamed bishops, while Christ appears flanked by censer-swinging angels and soldiers in the bottom row, watched by the figure of an abbess (probably the Abbess of Romsey when the piece was commissioned) who announces in a Latin 'bubble' that Christ has risen from his tomb.

St Michael and All Angels, Rycote, Oxfordshire

Rycote Chapel lies at the end of a dusty lane pitted with potholes and flanked by fields of corn. From the small shady car park you catch a glimpse of the stepped gable of the present house, all that remains of the fine Tudor mansion that once played host to Elizabeth I and Charles I, close to which stands the neat little chapel surrounded by trees. This is rural Oxfordshire at its best, tranquil and timeless in spite of the M40 only a couple of miles away.

The chapel at Rycote dates from the middle of the 15th century. Like many similar buildings, it was built to serve the spiritual needs of the large house that stood alongside and its particular attraction lies not simply in its setting, but in the fact that virtually none of its fittings have been altered since the last quarter of the 17th century.

The oldest feature at Rycote is the font, a circular 12th-century bowl that stands on an octagonal 15th-century base. If this originated at Rycote, it may be evidence that an earlier chapel stood on the site, evidence that might would seem to be supported in part by the finding of pieces of Early English carved stonework nearby.

The canopied font cover is 15th century, as is the simple wooden seating in the nave and chancel and the base of the *rood screen*.

From the early years of the 17th century comes the western gallery, as well as the original *reredos* which is now situated close to the west door on the north wall of the tower. Further into the nave the north wall also contains a fireplace within the third pew, the purpose and age of which is a subject of some conjecture. As a pew fireplace pure and simple it would be a very unusual feature in a 15th-century church. On the other hand, it would be equally unusual to find a fireplace from a later century built in a humble pew, when its obvious location would be in one of the grander pews nearer the chancel. Another possibility is that the fireplace might have been used to bake the wafers used for mass, but no definitive explanation has so far been arrived at.

The original 15th-century roof is still in place and from the upper level of the tower it is possible to look through a small window eastwards along the underside of the ridgeboard right to the gable at the far end. In the 17th century the roof was painted, and a small section at the western end has been restored to show gold stars on a blue background which gives a vivid impression of the remarkable effect this decor would have had on the chapel when it originally ran the full length of the roof.

The rood screen at Rycote survives in its lowest portion, which today forms the east wall of both the large pews at the eastern end of the nave. Inside the north pew a simple 15th-century door leads to the *rood loft* stairs which now lead up to the loft over the pew that was probably created to accommodate musicians. The wooden wall surrounding this loft consists of intricately decorated fretwork that was carefully restored earlier this century. The ceiling in the north pew is painted with stars and blue clouds. There is painted panelling on the north wall of this pew that originally showed four rows of oval pictures in three panels, most of which are obscured today.

On the other side of the nave the canopied southern

pew has been decorated with a design of eight-pointed stars. At the apex of the vaulting is a carved rose, similar in appearance to a Tudor rose. Charles I paid a visit to Rycote in 1625 and it is believed that the southern pew was constructed specially for this event. The northern pew is thought to have been built some fifteen years earlier to serve as the pew for the Norreys family; they came into the estate by marriage during the reign of Queen Elizabeth I.

The present reredos dates from 1682 and forms a handsome addition to the chapel. The quality of the carving has led to its being attributed to Grinling Gibbons, although there is no evidence to link him specifically with the Rycote reredos. All that can be said is that the work was undertaken by a craftsman of no mean ability. Above the two panels with semicircular arches that contain the Ten Commandments painted in gold is a beautifully carved winged cherub's head surmounting a *cartouche* bearing the word God in four languages: Hebrew, Greek, Latin and English.

The work of a 20th-century craftsman of similar accomplishments can also be found at Rycote, though less prominently displayed. On the south wall is a simple memorial plaque in memory of Colonel Alfred Hammersley, who did much to preserve the chapel. Look carefully and you will see it bears the initials of Eric Gill, the carver, engraver and typographer; he rarely signed work of this sort, but made a notable exception in this case.

Another tomb that attracts the visitor is the memorial stone in the floor of the nave to Margaret Tilly. Read the description of the good lady and form your opinion of what living with her might have been like.

Rycote and its chapel played an important part in the early life of Elizabeth I. At that time the house belonged to Sir John (later Lord) Williams, a man at the forefront of national politics in the turbulent years under Henry VIII and his three children. As Sheriff of Oxfordshire during the reign of Queen Mary he attended the burnings at the stake in Oxford of Latimer and Ridley in October 1555, and that of Cranmer a few months later in March 1556. Mary also made Williams one of the guardians of her stepsister Elizabeth and it was in this capacity that he entertained his future queen at Rycote, dying a year into her reign in 1559.

Following the marriage of Lord Williams's daughter, Marjorie, to Sir Henry Norreys, Rycote passed into the Norreys family. The queen had a great fondness for Sir Henry, whose father had been executed as the alleged lover of her mother Anne Boleyn. She made several visits to Rycote during her reign, her last being in 1592. Thirty-three years later, when Parliament and the court moved to Oxford to escape the plague in London, Charles I paid the visit that reputedly occasioned the building of the south pew.

Pre-dating both of these monarchs and the chapel itself is the huge yew tree that stands on its south side. No one knows for certain how old it is, but its immense girth speaks of centuries of growth. Some say it may have been planted to commemorate the coronation of King Stephen on 22 December 1135, others reckon it is considerably older than that.

There is one further point of interest about the yew. Take note if a tall woman appears by it while you're there. She hasn't been seen for some time and at first sight there is nothing very remarkable about her. It's only when she passes through the hedge or the small wooden office that you realize she is a ghost.

St Neot, St Neot, Cornwall

The parish of St Neot is the second largest in Cornwall, and the handsome church that dominates the attractive village nestling on the southern flank of Bodmin Moor is one of the best in the county. For anyone with an interest in medieval glass a visit is essential, for St Neot's has the finest late 15th- and early 16th- century glass in the West Country.

The church tower was built in the Decorated style, while the nave and south aisle date from a little later, in the 15th century. The north aisle was built a century after and, facing into the hillside, is significantly plainer; St Neot's was built to be admired from its southern aspect.

Just outside the church door the upright of a granite cross, elaborately decorated on all four faces, reminds the visitor of the early stirrings of Christianity in the area. There are records of a college of priests in the parish before the Norman Conquest and the cross, the best example in Cornwall and dating from the 10th century, confirms their presence and lasting influence.

The patron saint himself is of more than usual interest. There is some uncertainty as to whether St Neot was Celtic or Saxon. Tradition holds that at some stage his bones were moved to Huntingdonshire, giving rise to the town of St Neots. He is also linked with Alfred the Great. On the other side of the argument the existence of the cross by the church and the holy well (which we'll come to presently), not to mention the stories, largely Celtic in nature, told in one of the church windows about this remarkable saint suggest that Neot was a Celt through and through.

Inside the church his window in the north aisle is perhaps the first to make for; it is one of the most interesting and is unique in its subject matter, for in twelve panels it tells the legendary history of little Neot, who – at a height of just fifteen inches – must rank as the shortest saint of all time.

Moving from left to right and top to bottom the window shows Neot taking his holy vows and entering into the life of a monk; this included standing in the holy well named after him to read the psalter every day; according to some accounts he went as far as standing up to his neck in water to do this, but at fifteen inches high this can't have been hard to do. The story continues with an angel telling Neot about his source of sustenance, three fishes in the well, which would always remain there provided that he took only one each day to eat. Then Neot falls ill and his servant, hoping to rally him, returns from the well with two fishes. Neot tells him to take these back to the well where they are thrown into the water and restored to life. In the next episode brigands steal the little saint's oxen but he is able to continue his ploughing when stags nearby offer their services. The oxen then return to the saint and, in the final panel, St Neot is shown receiving the papal blessing.

The west window in the north aisle tells the story of a more familiar saint, St George, though he is shown undergoing considerably greater trials than taking on the dragon. This window also shows a dozen scenes from his life, in most of which poor St George comes off rather the worst. He is shown being executed twice, though restored to life after the first beheading by a thoughtful angel. After killing the dragon he is made to undergo a series of extremely gruesome tortures at the end of which his head is chopped off a second time.

At the eastern end of the south wall in the south aisle is a lovely window that tells the story of Noah in eight main compartments. The scenes have a vitality and naturalness rarely found in church glass and are reason enough in themselves for visiting St Neot's.

The east window over the altar in the Lady chapel of the south aisle is the Creation Window, the least restored in the church and generally held to be its best. Below the representation of different grades of angels in the 'heavenly league table' the window tells the story of the Creation in fifteen scenes from God's first plans to his command to Noah to build the ark. Along the way we see the familiar story of Adam and Eve and their dismissal from Paradise. Cain and Abel are there, too. The penultimate scene is interesting in detailing the death of Adam and the planting by Seth in his mouth of the seed from which the cross on Calvalry will eventually grow.

These are the windows of principal interest, but all of them are worth studying and most contain a good proportion of their original 15th- and 16th- century glass. Pick a sunny day to visit and the effect inside the church is all the more rewarding and uplifting.

While the windows are the church's major attraction, it has interesting Royalist connections stemming from the Civil War. At the east end of the north wall is a copy of a letter written by Charles I to the inhabitants of Cornwall in September 1643, which he commanded to be published and displayed in every church and chapel in the county. In it he thanks the Cornish for their loyal support and in return St Neot's, like many other churches in Cornwall, still displays its copy painted on a board.

St Neot's goes further, too. Every Oak Apple Day (29 May) the churchwardens place a fresh oak branch on the tower as a reminder of the future Charles II's escape from

St Peter's, Howden, is a large church with a tall central tower that rises magnificently over the town.

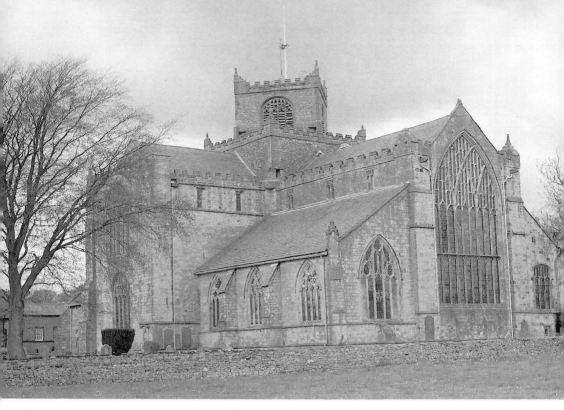

The Priory church of St Mary and St Michael, Cartmel (above), is one of the undiscovered secrets of north-west England while the Priory church of St Mary Magdalene, Lanercost (below), provided a secret resting place in the border wars of the Middle Ages.

the Battle of Worcester by hiding in an oak tree. There it stays all year until the next anniversary and the arrival of a fresh bough.

Three hundred yards from the church, in a meadow up a lane in the middle of the village, is St Neot's Well, one of several in Cornwall. As might be expected from the somewhat slight proportions of its patron saint, this is traditionally empowered with strengthening delicate children.

St Peter and St Paul, Salle, Norfolk

Salle is the neighbouring parish to Cawston (see pages 72–4), and together the two churches rank among the very best in the country.

Salle, like Cawston, owes its existence to the wool trade and to the patronage of three local families: the Boleyns, the Fountaines and the Briggs, who throughout the 15th century lavished their wealth on creating a magnificent church, larger than many cathedrals, to the enduring glory of God.

The richly decorated west tower beckons the visitor to the small village where the population has seldom exceeded more than a few hundred. Built between 1422 and 1461 (except for the top storey, that was added at the end of the 15th century) the tower stands 111 feet high. On either side of the west door two beautifully carved feathered angels swinging censers, and fourteen finely worked coats of arms, herald the rich decoration that lies inside. The empty niches above the door and to each side probably held figures of Christ and the two patron saints, all of which presumably disappeared during the Reformation when so many of Salle's artistic treasures were confiscated or destroyed. Raise your eyes, and you'll see the splendid tracery of the 'sound holes' in the centre of the tower.

The church has two fine porches, the one on the north having an intricate vaulted roof with a central boss

214

depicting the Last Judgement. The south porch was a gift of the Brigg family, whose arms appear above the central niche.

Once inside the church the magnificent font immediately catches the eye. In spite of suffering grievous damage it is still a potent expression of the sculptor's creative genius both in the font itself and its tall graceful cover. This is a seven-sacrament font, of which East Anglia has by far the largest surviving collection in the country. The panels show, in order from the south-west corner: the sacraments of the altar, holy orders, baptism, confirmation, penance, matrimony and unction, with the eighth panel depicting the Crucifixion. An unusual feature at Salle is that below seven of the panels are angels holding symbols corresponding with the sacrament above.

Looking up the nave, the church is graced by one of the loveliest Perpendicular arcades in the country. Tall slender columns rise to the airy *clerestory* and the handsome, originally painted (as the remaining traces show), roof with its fine bosses.

The lovely 15th-century 'wine-glass' pulpit, however, still bears much of its original colouring. Two centuries later it was successfully adapted to conform with the three-decker style by the addition of a seat for the parish clerk and a reading desk.

In the floor of the north transept lies the memorial brass to Thomas Rose and his wife, showing their eight sons and four daughters. He was another wealthy wool merchant who used part of his fortune to construct the transept. This is one of the many fine brasses found throughout the church.

The doorway in the north-west corner of the north aisle leads up to the Lady chapel over the north porch; for a long time this served as a schoolroom. In the corresponding corner of the south aisle is the stairway leading to the room over the south porch which may have acted as a treasury. The aisle itself contains a number of memorials to members of the Brigg family, one of whom, Thomas Brigg, added the south transept. This, like the north transept, has a beautiful panelled roof, which, it is claimed, was taken as a model for that in the lobby of the House of Lords. The builder of the transept is depicted in the east window with his two wives, both named Margaret.

Moving towards the chancel, the screen bears the saw marks where its upper part was cut off in the 16th century. Four of the twelve Apostles are painted in the outer panels, with fragments of the Creed inscribed above them, and it has been suggested that there may have originally been a return screen on each side with figures of the eight remaining Apostles. At no time do the four panels north and south appear to have been painted.

Above the chancel itself the roof is decorated with nine exquisitely carved bosses showing scenes from Christ's life, beginning at the western end with the Annunciation and ending with the Ascension. The twenty-five oak stalls are attractively carved as well, with human heads on the south side and animals and birds on the north. The chancel also contains the best of the church's stained glass, with several of the figures in the east window on the south side repositioned there from the tracery of the east window.

St Mary, Selborne, Hampshire

4 MILES SOUTH OF ALTON, ON B3006

In St Mary's churchyard, on the north side of the chancel, a simple headstone inscribed 'G.W. 1793' marks the grave of Gilbert White, the naturalist, who is as intimately associated with this church as William Wordsworth is with St Oswald's, Grasmere.

White was born in Selborne and, after becoming an Oxford don, returned to his native village in 1755 as a curate. Here he wrote the book that has won him everlasting fame: *The Natural History and Antiquities of Selborne*, which was published in 1789.

St Mary's stands near Gilbert White's house, The Wakes, which is now a museum and memorial library dedicated to him. Seen from the village green (known as the Plestor), the church is almost hidden by a massive yew tree reckoned to be anything from 800 to 1,400 years old. With a girth of over twenty-six feet at shoulder height, it is still going strong; two hundred years ago when White was alive the same measurement was a mere twenty-three feet.

St Mary's is mainly Norman-Transitional and Early English in style, though considerably restored in the last century by Gilbert White's great-nephew, William White. The nave has large Norman pillars that support pointed Transitional arches. The chancel, which was probably built at much the same time, contains one of several memorials to Gilbert White. In this case it is a painting

217

serving as a *reredos* which has been attributed to the Flemish artist Jan Mostaert, who probably painted it about 1516. Gilbert White's brother and publisher, Benjamin, presented it to the church in his memory in 1793.

In 1920 the south window that shows St Francis of Assisi preaching to the birds was installed as a further memorial to mark the bicentenary of the naturalist's birth. The church, the great yew and the vicarage where White was born all appear.

Until 1735 St Mary's had three untuned bells in its tower. In that year they were melted down to be recast as four and at the same time Sir Simeon Stuart, who lived locally, donated another named after his daughter Clare. As Gilbert White recorded, the people of Selborne were grateful to him on two counts. 'The day of the arrival of this tuneable peal,' he wrote, 'was observed as an high festival in the village and rendered more joyous by an order from the donor that the treble bell should be fixed bottom upward in the ground and filled with punch, of which all present were invited to partake.'

St Peter, Shorwell, Isle of Wight

Lying in a wooded valley, Shorwell boasts three manor houses along with the largely Perpendicular church of St Peter. One of these houses, named Northcourt, was the home of Sir John Leigh, who proved to be such a generous benefactor to St Peter's in the early 17th century.

The church took on most of its present shape in the middle of the 14th century, with the tower the last section to be built.

St Peter's is a church 'collector's' emporium, quite dark inside and full of interesting things. The pews are crowded with *poppy-heads* carved by Sir Henry Gordon towards the end of the last century and added to the 17th-century pews.

The Perpendicular stone pulpit governs the layout of the central seats in the church; they run east-west, giving the interior the appearance of a college chapel. It probably dates from the middle of the 15th century, when the arcades were constructed and the church was radically reshaped. The canopy over the pulpit and the iron hourglass stand are both fine examples of Jacobean work, and may well count among the many gifts made to the church by Sir John Leigh.

The vestry at the west end of the south aisle formerly served the very different purpose of a gunroom, one of the very last to survive in a parish church. A blocked-up arch in the west wall under the window provided access for the gun and there was a separate door, blocked as well, from the outside.

Through the arcades visitors can see the large 15th-century wall painting of St Christopher over the north door which is one of Shorwell's greatest attractions. This is unusual in that it shows various scenes from the saint's life. In the centre is the familiar image of the saint bearing the infant Christ across a river towards a small hermitage. On one side St Christopher is seen renouncing the Devil, who is shown with the pointed ears of a satyr and wearing an odd-looking crown. The other side shows the martyrdom of St Christopher in a manner similar to that of St Sebastian, who was killed by arrows. The whole painting is filled with fascinating details from the range of fish depicted to the signalling shown between a ship's mast-head and beacon station.

The roof beam over the chancel dates from the 15th century as well and though not a *rood beam* like those frequently found in medieval churches it still carries the finely carved figures of Christ flanked by St Michael and St Gabriel. The corbels on which it rests show the figures of Sin and Death.

St Peter's is also filled with a fascinating collection of monuments and brasses. The oldest is a brass in the floor of the chancel commemorating Richard Bethell, a former vicar who died in 1518. The most imposing monument is quite rightly that of Sir John Leigh, whose generous gifts and endowments include the pulpit canopy, the font cover, the spire and much of the furnishing in the church. He is shown dressed in armour, kneeling at a faldstool (a movable desk for kneeling at) in the north aisle. Behind him is the poignant figure of his great-grandson, nine-month-old Barnabas Leigh, who died shortly after him; they were buried in the same tomb.

At the east end of the north aisle is a striking brass memorial to the two wives of Sir John Leigh's son, also named Barnabas. One died the mother of fifteen children, the other died childless, and both are shown with a foot on a central skull and one hand on a large ring held from above by a lace-cuffed hand.

Among its literary treasures St Peter's has a fine copy of Cranmer's Bible from 1541, the first Bible the church owned and one that was duly chained to a desk – as the rivets in its binding show.

St Mary, Sompting, West Sussex

Set on the southern slope of the South Downs with a fine view over Worthing, St Mary's, Sompting, is unique among English churches in retaining its Saxon tower capped with a four-sided shingled roof that is the nearest Saxon builders came to erecting a spire. The top of each of the four stone gables of the tower rises to a point, so that the roof between them forms a diamond pattern. Towers of this design are common in the Rhineland and are accordingly described by the name Rhenish helm. The shingles that act as roofing material are oblong strips of cleft oak and beneath them the original Saxon roofing timbers are still in place. The small windows near the top are typically Saxon, too.

The tower arch is off-centre, due to an altar which once stood against its east wall. This is a good example of a Saxon arch; crude but robust, it carries the influence of arches formerly built by the Roman inhabitants of the area.

The rest of the church was rebuilt in the 12th century by the Templars, the order of crusading monks whose power and wealth grew steadily during the Middle Ages until their suppression early in the 14th century. The nave and chancel were reconstructed along the lines of the original Saxon plan, the walls following the lines of those of the tower. The north and south transepts were added to serve initially as chapels, walled off from the rest

222

of the church. When St Mary's passed from the control of the Templars to the more favoured crusader order of the Knights of St John, the chapels were opened to the local congregation, while the new patrons built themselves a chapel north of the tower (which stands in ruins today). The patronage was returned to the Knights of St John in 1963.

No chancel arch separates the nave from the chancel here. In the south wall, close to the altar, is the *piscina*, adorned at the top by two strips of Saxon carving. The south wall also contains a blocked-up opening which may once have connected with the south transept which lies at a lower level. The limestone *reredos* behind the altar is Victorian, as are the stained-glass windows.

Both transepts were originally conceived as churches in miniature with their own little chancels and sacristies (in the north transept the southern of the two small chapels at the eastern end would have acted as the chancel).

The font that stands in the small chancel of the south chapel is a fitting symbol of the church's long history and active present, comprising as it does the original 12th-century bowl of Sussex marble standing on a modern pillar.

St Edmund, Southwold, Suffolk

Together with Blythburgh, this is one of the great churches of east Suffolk. Totally rebuilt with great splendour in the 15th century, it replaced an earlier church that had been destroyed by fire and is consequently homogenous in design and construction, most of the work having been completed by about 1460, with only the wonderful screen dating from the end of that century.

Viewed from the outside the church presents a pleasing harmony of elegant proportions and delicate ornamentation, achieved from the combination of stone and flint flushwork panels. The tower, in particular, benefits from the use of flushwork panels on its buttresses and in the lozenge decoration around the parapet. On the west face is a chequerboard design, which is repeated on the sides of the superb south porch.

The 'glasshouse' effect so sought after by masons of the Perpendicular period is wonderfully achieved by the lofty *clerestory* and the generously proportioned windows of the aisles.

Around the arch of the west window runs a Latin inscription (with each letter crowned) to St Edmund, the church's patron saint, asking 'St Edmund, pray for us'. A monogrammed 'M' representing the initial of the Virgin Mary appears in a set of lovely panels around the south porch, along with others bearing a more complicated design forming her full name, Mary. The room over the

224

south porch has been used as a store-room for church valuables, as an arsenal and as a schoolroom.

The church reinforces its stately external appearance inside through the tall, slender piers of the nave and the hammer-beam roof that runs from east to west giving an impression of complete harmony and space. Most of the glass is modern, due to the damage caused by air raids in the last war, but there are the remains of the original painted and gilded woodwork to add authentic colour to the interior.

The portion of the roof over the chancel is painted, with the colour applied to the angels at the base of the rafters highlighting the delicate details of their carving.

Above the screen the roof is decorated as a 'canopy of honour' with twenty panels painted with blue backgrounds spangled with golden stars. A painted angel appears in each panel as well, some bearing emblems of Christ's passion, others carrying scrolls with words from the 'Benedictus'. Inscriptions from the 'Te Deum' run beneath them.

Of all the painted work in the church, the screen that stretches right across the church, decorated with magnificent figure paintings, is the most striking and glorious, ranking among the most beautiful surviving screens in England. Apart from its colouring the Southwold screen is famous for the exquisite 'gesso' plaster-work decorations which are used extensively on the small buttresses, in the fillets and traceries of the panels and on their backgrounds. The central section of the screen shows the best concentration of design and painting. This shows the Apostles. The northern section in front of the Holy Trinity chapel has representations of the choir of angels, while that on the southern side in front of the Lady chapel shows the prophets. The Ten Commandments are painted along the plain top of the screen where it runs in front of the two chapels, and at one time a narrow

225

rood-loft would have surmounted the whole screen. Like virtually every other rood in the country, this disappeared in the 16th century.

The fine pre-Reformation pulpit was repainted in 1930 thanks to the people of Southwold, Long Island, who were the descendants of 17th-century settlers from Southwold, Suffolk. Supported on a slender pillar, the pulpit still had traces of its 15th-century colouring in the 19th century, which presumably made the task of recolouring some-what easier ninety years later.

In the chancel the choir with its canopied stalls and return stalls resembles a smaller version of a cathedral choir. There are some fine carvings on the arm-rests of the stalls, showing a variety of grotesque subjects. Two other interesting carvings are the bosses in the roof of the Lady chapel which represent Mary Tudor, Henry VIII's sister, and her second husband, Charles Brandon, Duke of Suffolk, who for a time lived four miles from Southwold at Henham. The duke's beard and the duchess's elaborate hair-do obviously made an impression on the carver.

On the north arch of the tower stands another carved figure, known as 'Jack-smite-the-clock' or 'Southwold Jack', who strikes a bell with a short battle-axe to mark the start of each service. In addition to his weaponry, he is shown as a perfect representation of a foot soldier at the end of the 15th century, exactly like those who fought in the Wars of the Roses. The details of his armour, footwear and clothing are authentic and his face, with unshaven chin and blood-flecked eyes, adds further realistic touches.

St Nicholas, Stanford-on-Avon, Northamptonshire

15 MILES NORTH-WEST OF NORTHAMPTON, OFF B5414

St Nicholas stands on the Northamptonshire bank of the River Avon opposite Stanford Hall, which was built as the seat of Sir Roger Cave at the turn of the 18th century.

A substantial Norman church once stood on the site, and probably a Saxon one before that. However, the present building dates from the first half of the 14th century when the Abbot of Selby, to whom the manor of Stanford belonged, appointed his nephew, Alan de Aslaghby, as its vicar in 1307. Influenced by the enthusiasm for the light, elegant churches of the Continent and Middle East, reports of which filtered back with returning crusaders, he set about restyling his new church in the first year of his incumbency. The nave, aisles and tower were entirely rebuilt, work on the last being cut short by the Black Death which broke out in the middle of the 14th century. Only the chancel remained standing, though its windows were enlarged.

In 1909 the ceiling of the chancel was taken down and revealed early Norman oak roof timbers, formed from the lightly trimmed boughs of a massive tree. The stalls overlooked by the low window in the south wall are also made from solid oak, trimmed with an adze, and may date from the same period. The linenfold oak panelling

227

is Elizabethan, though, having come from the original Stanford Hall which was demolished in 1689.

The east window, well known for its lovely medieval glass, reflects an interesting piece of ecclesiastical detective work. The top half belongs to the reign of Edward II in the first quarter of the 14th century. The five lower panels are from a later period, but were missing for several hundred years – until 1932, when they were found in an old chest in Stanford Hall. When placed in position in the window they were found to fit exactly into the spaces in the lower lights, which had been filled with plain glass presumably since their removal, which may have come about during the Civil War.

The north aisle of the nave has some fine monuments commemorating various members of the Cave family whose fine armorial bearings can be seen around the walls. The south aisle contains the figure of a priest in a decorated recess. His vestments and the decoration surrounding him point to the 14th century, and it seems almost certain that this is an effigy of Alan de Aslaghby himself.

In the midst of this delightful medieval church the superb early Renaissance-style organ case in the western gallery forms a perfect complement. The organ is one of the most interesting to be found in any parish church, not simply because so few organs survive from before the Restoration of Charles II in 1660, but because this organ originally belonged to his father, Charles I, and stood in the Chapel Royal at Whitehall Palace. On top of the organ can be seen a bishop's mitre surmounted by a crown, reflecting Charles I's unswayable belief in the divine right of kings which brought about his execution in Whitehall. (Interestingly, Archbishop Laud, who had been executed four years earlier for working towards the same end as his monarch, had once been vicar of Stanford.)

Following the execution of Charles I, Oliver Cromwell sold his effects and the organ was bought by Magdalen College, Oxford. However, it was found to be too small for the college's requirements and was sold to Sir Thomas Cave shortly afterwards to be installed in his church beside the River Avon at Stanford, where ironically archbishop and king were symbolically reunited.

St Mary the Virgin, Steeple Ashton, Wiltshire

At one time Steeple Ashton was known by the name of Staple Ashton, on account of the wool market established there by charter in 1397. As with so many late medieval churches, it was the prosperity brought by the wool trade that led to the building of the ornately battlemented and pinnacled parish church in that final flourishing of English church building. The tower came first, followed by the nave, aisles, east chapels and porches. Only the small chancel remained from the earlier church, but this too was replaced by the present one in 1853.

As a brass tablet at the west end of the church records, building work began in 1480 with the aisles paid for by a couple of wealthy wool-traders and their wives, and the cost of the rest of the church shared among the other parishioners. Unfortunately this prosperity was comparatively short-lived and plans that may have existed to vault the nave in the same way as the aisles and chapels were never carried out; nor was the old Early English chancel replaced with a new one more in keeping with the grand Perpendicular building that now stood beside it. In 1670 the tall spire (186 feet) was struck by lightning and collapsed, killing two men working on it at the time

230

and causing a certain amount of damage to the south aisle.

In place of the vaulting that may or may not have been intended, the nave is roofed with oak and plaster in the pattern of fan-vaulting, rich in pendent bosses surrounded by carvings of animals, cornucopia, eagles and horses' heads.

The north aisle roof, in contrast, is finely vaulted with the vaulting springing from canopied niches with male and female figures carved on the *corbels*. There are remains of medieval glass in the finely traceried windows.

The wall of the Lady chapel at the east end of the north aisle has an interesting *palimpsest* which shows Queen Anne with her husband Prince George, accompanied by two bishops, standing beside a large pair of scales in one of which sits the Holy Bible. The caption above suggests that the other (now missing) probably contained the Devil and the Pope.

Whereas the north aisle was built by Robert Long and his wife, the south aisle was a gift of Walter Lucas and his wife Maud. Though less impressive than the north aisle chapel, that in the south aisle contains some interesting old glass. In the south aisle the white rose of York can also be seen in the glass along with the white boar and rayed sun, both of which were symbols of Richard III. Richard was killed at the Battle of Bosworth in 1485, which indicates that the glass must pre-date his downfall. Three shields shown in the glass of the north aisle are those of St George, St Andrew and probably St Swithun. The destruction of the rest of the glass is usually laid at the door of Sir William Waller, a Parliamentary commander during the Civil War who had a fearsome reputation for defacing churches.

The south porch at Steeple Ashton is particularly impressive, having a fine vaulted roof with a great carved central boss depicting the Assumption.

The 17th-century sundial would appear to have been good value for money; according to the church accounts for 1636 it cost ten shillings!

St Mary, Stoke D'Abernon, Surrey

Within a century of St Augustine's arrival in southern England in 597, simple Saxon churches began to be built throughout the south-east of England. St Mary's, Stoke D'Abernon is one of the few of these to have retained a significant portion of its original structure; in this case the south wall as far as the porch, and what is left of the apse above the chancel ceiling.

For five hundred years the church stood unaltered. The blocked doorway twelve feet up in the south wall probably gave access by a wooden stairway to a gallery constructed for the local lord of the manor, making Stoke d'Abernon the earliest example of an English church with such a feature. When change did come about in the closing years of the 12th century, it was to enlarge the church by building the north aisle; two pointed arches and a pillar from this work survive. The faded painted crucifix on the pillar probably dates from the same time.

To the north of the chancel arch is a statue of the Madonna and Child made in northern Italy at the turn of the 16th century. Close by stands the 17th-century lectern, unusual for its twisted oak column set on an elm base. The imposing Elizabethan pulpit made from walnut is also unusual in its seven-sided design. Presented to the church by Sir Francis Vincent, it carries his coat of arms on the back panel. Beside the pulpit is a 17th-century hour-glass, which would have been the focal point for

233

apprehensive congregations in the days when preachers were liable to let the sands of time run all too liberally.

The church chest near the pulpit was made around the turn of the 13th century, and originally stored vessels and vestments. It also acted as a collecting box to raise funds for the crusades that were undertaken at that time, and may be one of the chests that were ordered to be placed in churches in 1199 for this purpose.

As the plan of the church shows, the chancel was constructed along an axis that is four degrees to the north of that of the nave, a divergence accounted for by changes in the calendar, and hence the position of dawn on particular dates, that took place over the six hundred years that separated them. Built in the middle of the 13th century, the chancel replaced the Saxon apse with a splendid vaulted and decorated ceiling typical of the period. It seems likely that the work was undertaken at the instigation of Sir John D'Abernon to contain his tomb, later to be joined by those of his son and grandson. To begin with there was no east window, the east wall being adorned instead by a mural depicting the Adoration of the Lamb. However, a shortage of light prompted the creation of a large east window early in the following century and the only part of the original painting still visible is in the top right-hand corner of the wall.

When Sir John D'Abernon commissioned his final resting-place I doubt if he reckoned on the fact that seven hundred years later his memorial brass would be the oldest surviving one in the country. Dating from 1277, this is magnificently worked, still retains traces of its blue enamelling on the shield and is a good six feet long. It shows Sir John dressed in chainmail and holding his spear, unlike his son who is shown beside him wearing the half-plate armour of his day, half a century later.

At the east end of the north aisle, through the 17th-century Italian wrought-iron gates, lies the *chantry* chapel founded by Sir John Norbury – apparently as an expression of his thanks for returning safely from the Battle of Bosworth (1485) in which Richard III lost his crown. This contains the figures of Sir Thomas Vincent (father of the donor of the pulpit) and his wife Lady Jane on the north wall, while along the east wall reclines their daughter-in-law Lady Sarah Vincent who died at the age of thirty-seven, already the mother of seven children. Her offspring are shown praying along the plinth of her tomb. In the south-east corner of the chapel is a Roman stone funerary casket dating from the 2nd century AD, which contains the ashes of Sir Edgar Vincent, British Ambassador to Germany from 1920 to 1926. It's interesting that on the south wall of the chapel the memorial brass to Sir Thomas Lyfelde shows his wife Frances together with their daughter Jane, the same Lady Jane who married Thomas Vincent and is commemorated in the monument on the north wall.

Another lady made her mark at Stoke D'Abernon for a rather different reason. This was the aptly named Joanna Sturdy, who practised the craft of bell-founding at Croydon in the middle of the 15th century. She was responsible for casting one of the six bells at St Mary's.

St John the Baptist, Stokesay, Shropshire

Although St John's could never be described as remarkable, its history justifies a visit – as does its location.

The church was built in the 12th century to act as a chapel to the castle, one of the earliest fortified manor houses in England and notable for the size of the windows in its great hall and its gracious oak-panelled drawing-room, both of which are features not usually associated with medieval 'castles' along the Welsh marches.

During the Civil War Stokesay Castle escaped serious damage when the Royalist garrison surrendered after offering only brief resistance. The church fared less well, however, and much of it was destroyed by cannon fire in 1646 when Royalist cavalry took refuge inside. What makes it especially interesting is that in 1654 the damage was repaired and the church rebuilt, making it one of the few churches built during the period of Cromwell's Commonwealth. The tower was added a decade later, after Charles II had been restored to the throne, which provides a further interesting historical perspective.

Below the Georgian gallery are half a dozen early pews that survived the Civil War engagement. These are fitted with ledges that served as foot-rests, not book-rests as one might imagine. When the church was first built there was no floor and the ground surface consisted of rough earth

and stones. The font probably escaped the damage suffered by the rest of the church and its plainness suggests
that it, too, is of considerable age.

From the latter half of the 17th century come the box
pews, the canopied pews in the chancel and the pulpit, all
of which were installed a few years after the Restoration
in 1660. The chancel was restored at the same time, as the
date 1664 on the supporting beam confirms. The arms on
the *corbels* are those of the Baldwyn family who occupied
the castle at the time.

St Mary, Stow-in-Lindsey, Lincolnshire

The known history of this church reaches back to before the Norman Conquest and its mythical history begins even earlier, at some point in the latter half of the 7th century. According to legend St Etheldreda stopped here *en route* from Northumbria (fleeing her husband King Ecgfrith, with whom she must have had a pretty serious disagreement), thrust her ash staff into the ground, whereupon it burst into leaf to provide her with shelter. St Etheldreda moved on to Ely where she founded the cathedral in 673 and her husband, so the legend says, respectfully built a church at Stow to commemorate the miraculous event.

It sounds a bit far-fetched, especially as there is no hard evidence that St Etheldreda actually visited this particular Stow (there is another, in the southern part of the county). However, two hundred years later Stow lay at the centre of a sizeable area of land belonging to the Saxon bishops of Dorchester-on-Thames, and Bishop Aelfnoth decided in 975 that a minster should be built to serve this part of his diocese, Stow being the chosen site.

Parts of his structure survive in the lower sections of the transepts and the crossings, but the bulk of Bishop Aelfnoth's church was destroyed by fire and had to be rebuilt in the middle of the the 11th century by his successor, Bishop Eadnoth II, who received financial assistance from Leofric, Earl of Mercia, and his wife Lady Godiva.

By the time that Duke William of Normandy landed at Hastings in 1066 St Mary's had assumed much of its present shape, making it one of the largest and most impressive pre-Conquest churches in the country – all the more significant in that it retains its original cruciform plan with a central tower and equally proportioned crossing arches.

The nave was built on the instruction of Remigius, the first Norman bishop of Dorchester-on-Thames, before he moved his see to Lincoln in 1073. His intention had been to turn Stow into a Benedictine monastery, but that scheme was short-lived and from the last quarter of the 11th century it became what it is today, a parish church.

A century later the Saxon chancel was replaced by a more elaborate Norman one and come the 15th century the Saxon tower was partly taken down, to be replaced by the present one in the Perpendicular style.

It must also be acknowledged that much of the splendid work we see today is due to the restoration carried out by John Loughborough Pearson (the designer of Truro Cathedral) in 1863–5. The tiling on the floors might be questioned, but he was responsible for restoring the roofs to their original pitch and rebuilding the vaulting in the choir.

One effect of repitching the roofs was to reveal the great ledge above the tower arches in the nave and transepts which was created when the Saxon tower was taken down to be replaced by the present one. The nave windows, though early Norman in date, show strong Saxon influences in their large upright stones.

The font, Norman or Early English, is remarkable in its decoration, for none of the images carved on it is a specifically Christian symbol.

239

At the crossing you can see the two styles of arches built to support the two different towers. The outer, round arches, supported the original Saxon tower, while the inner, pointed ones were built to support the present Perpendicular tower.

The south wall of the south transept has three windows of three different periods, beginning with the narrow slit window built by the Saxon builders. Above this is a round Norman window, which probably dates from the same period as the chancel. And from the 13th century comes the two-light Gothic window.

The north transept has a very fine Saxon doorway that now leads into the vestry. This was part of the original Saxon church, probably leading into an aisle or chapel. It is built of single stones that reach right through the wall, the ones on the left being arranged in the characteristic Saxon long-and-short pattern.

The spacious and richly decorated chancel has been considerably, though it is believed accurately, restored. The vaulting has been replaced, the east wall above the arcade was largely rebuilt, replacing a Gothic window built in the 13th century. There is a very early memorial inscription in English (part of it written in mirror-fashion) on the south side of the chancel and on the south pier of the chancel arch is a piece of graffiti showing an oared sailing ship – the earliest known drawing of a Viking ship in England, dating from the late 10th or early 11th century.

St Clement, Terrington, Norfolk

Previous churches stood on the site now occupied by this fine Perpendicular church, of which parts of the Early English building have been incorporated into the present structure, which was erected in the latter half of the 14th century. Built of Barnack stone brought by barge from Northamptonshire, St Clement's has a fine west front, a greatly admired *clerestory* and a detached tower, which together with its other noble features have earned it the title of Cathedral of the Marshland.

It was the nature of the foundations that probably accounted for the building of the tower separately from the rest of church, at the north-west corner. It's thought that the original plan was to build it in the centre, but when this presented too great a mass to be supported, the current location was adopted. In addition to housing the bells, the tower of St Clement's also provided refuge to the parishioners on at least two occasions in the 17th century when the sea broke through the coastal defences and inundated the surrounding area. This happened in 1613, and again in 1670, and the people of Terrington had to climb into the tower where they were brought provisions by boat from King's Lynn.

On either side of the west door are two crosses marked when the church was consecrated and similar ones were inscribed on the inside of the west wall in much the same position, though only one is now visible. There

241

are also canopied niches for the figures of St Clement and St Christopher, which in 1887 were found hidden behind two buttresses and are now housed in the vestry on the south side, and there's a smaller niche too above the door.

Inside the church, seven large niches in the west arch of the *lantern* originally contained the figures of saints. In the north and south transepts are two impressive Jacobean tablets bearing the Lord's Prayer and the Creed, both mounted in their original positions.

Entering the chancel there are three stone altar slabs set in the floor, each marked by five crosses; a fourth slab lies under the present altar. In 1879, Professor J.B. Lightfoot, the then rector and subsequent Bishop of Durham, carried out much needed restoration in the chancel and also built the vicar's vestry which lies through the Early English doorway. From this period come the *sedilia* and double *piscina* now situated on the south side of the sanctuary, where the altar was raised to make room for the vault constructed beneath it for the Bentinck family.

In 1788 the oak screen was erected to support a gallery where the choir and village band could be accommodated. However, it also served the practical purpose of cutting down draughts from the north, west and south doors.

Terrington's 15th-century font is surmounted by a remarkable *tabernacle* cover from a century later, which has opening doors that reveal painted scenes from the life of Christ – his baptism, fasting and temptation. There's also an inscription in Latin which means in translation, 'The Father (revealed) by the voice, the Son by the body, the spirit by the dove.'

Holy Cross, Tetcott, Devon

5 MILES SOUTH OF HOLSWORTHY, OFF A388

Tetcott church is almost certainly the most obscure in this book. Tucked away in south Devon, close to the Cornish border, it is a plain rustic building constructed in the late 13th century with the addition of a tower, east window and south chapel two centuries later.

However, Holy Cross has a unique fascination through its close connections with the Arscott family, lords of the manor from the early 1500s until the late 1700s, and with one Arscott in particular, the last and most extraordinary of the line, John Arscott, who died in 1788 and is said still to haunt the church and nearby house.

John Arscott was a strange chap in anyone's book, living a life of boundless eccentricity in which his chief passion was hunting. He kept a tame toad whom he named 'Old Dowty', which answered to its master's call and took food from his table. There were rumours in the neighbourhood that the toad played familiar to his master's wizard, but any prospect of their collaboration in black magic was nipped in the bud when 'Old Dowty' was killed by a pet raven.

The squire was fond of a strange selection of animals. He used to carry a bottle of flies to feed the spiders in church – where he regularly threw apples at the parson. At home he lived for many years with a lady named Thomasina Spry, though they never had any children.

Theirs must have been an odd household, made all the

243

more peculiar by the presence of Black John, Arscott's dwarf jester and probably the last jester in England. He would entertain his master in a variety of unusual ways. Recalling a dream in which he had seen himself in Hell, he was asked what it had been like, and replied, 'Much as here at Tetcott, with the gentlefolk nearest the fire.' One of his party pieces, of which there were many unsavoury examples, consisted of lowering a live mouse down his gullet and then drawing it back up from his stomach! His grave lies in the churchyard at Tetcott.

If local tradition is to be believed his master can still be seen there at his favourite pastime, as an 18th-century ballad recalls:

When the full moon is shining as clear as day,
John Arscott still hunteth the country, they say,
You may see him on Blackbird, and hear in full cry
The pack from Pencarrow to Dazzard go by.

The memorial stone to twenty-five-year-old Flavinius, standard bearer of a Roman cavalry regiment, offers a dramatic glimpse into early English history in St Andrew's, Hexham (above left). There is also Roman masonry in Saxon Church, Escomb (above right).

The Minster church of St John the Evangelist, Beverley (below), is one of the most beautiful Gothic churches in Europe.

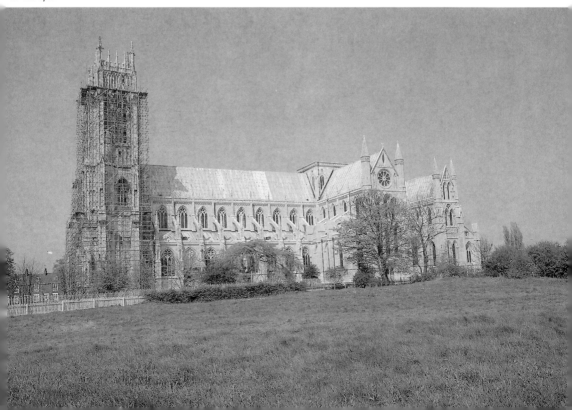

A pleasing West-Riding church, St Luke and All Saints, Darrington, is built of local Tadcaster limestone.

St Mary the Virgin, Tewkesbury, Gloucestershire

According to tradition, a monk of the 7th century named Theoc built a cell for himself on the east bank of the River Avon close to the point where it joins the Severn and on the site of the ancient town of Tewkesbury. By the year 715 Benedictine monks had arrived and built themselves a monastery, though no trace of this remains.

The present abbey is Norman and gloriously so, the second largest parish church in England and possessing the largest Norman tower and doorway (at the west end). Interestingly, the ground plan was almost identical to that drawn up for Westminster Abbey, but where the latter has been significantly altered, Tewkesbury has remained unashamedly Norman in feel throughout its history. In the 14th century the only significant additions to the Norman plans were made when the wonderful *lierne* vaulting was added to the whole building and the *ambulatory* with the attached group of apsidal chapels was constructed.

The abbey witnessed the Battle of Tewkesbury, fought on what is still known as Bloody Meadow, in May 1471. It was the scene of further fighting itself after defeated Lancastrian troops fled inside seeking sanctuary, only to be put to the sword by the Yorkist troops led by Edward

IV. It took a month for the building to be purged of this bloodshed and for reconsecration to take place.

In 1539 the townspeople succeeded in buying the church from Henry VIII for £453, that being the agreed value of the lead and bells which would otherwise have been sold. This they achieved on the grounds that the nave of the abbey church had served as their parish church since its foundation.

Following a familiar pattern in medieval churches, the accretions of 18th-century galleries and box pews were removed in the 19th century, which started the process of returning this great church to its original state.

On the outside the west front of the abbey has a magnificent sevenfold Norman arch, sixty-five feet high and the largest of its kind in the country. The present Perpendicular-style window replaces a 14th-century one blown down in 1661, which in turn took the place of the original Norman arrangement that probably consisted of several smaller round-headed windows.

Moving round to the south side, you come across the remains of the ruined cloister; it measured eighty feet square. There was once a Lady chapel at the eastern end of the church, but this was probably pulled down to make way for a larger one – which in the event was never completed.

Inside the church, the view up the nave with its fourteen massive columns nineteen feet round and rising over thirty feet high to support the 14th-century fan-vaulting is one of the most impressive in the country. Running along the intersection of the ribs of the vaulting is an interesting series of bosses. Those along the centre are arranged in three groups of five and depict scenes from the life of Christ: his early life, Holy Week and the triumph of the Resurrection.

Originally there would have been a *pulpitum* dividing the western part of the abbey (used by the people as their parish church) from the east end (that served the monks). This would have stood to the west of the present oak screen and the second pillars west of the screen carry marks of the spiral staircases that would have led to the *rood loft* on top of the stone screen.

Beyond the screen the choir is a masterpiece of Decorated arches and vaulting, below which are the celebrated windows that contain some of the best 14th-century glass in England; two of the windows show knights dressed in 14th-century armour.

In the floor of the choir a brass plate with a Latin inscription marks the burial place of Edward, the young Prince of Wales, who fell at the Battle of Tewkesbury. His is one of several tombs and monuments with great historical or artistic interest that rank Tewkesbury second only to Westminster in this respect.

Grouped around the choir are several of the most outstanding monuments in the abbey. On the north side of the altar lie the alabaster effigies of Hugh Despenser and his wife Elizabeth Montacute beneath a splendid late Decorated canopy. It was they who were chiefly responsible for the 14th-century alterations and additions to the abbey. Next to them is Abbot Parker's chantry, built over the tomb of the abbey's founder, Robert FitzHamon, which was built in the later Perpendicular style. Perhaps the most striking monument is the Beauchamp chapel, built by Isabella Despenser in memory of her husband Richard Beauchamp. This incredibly ornate canopied structure took sixteen years to complete, and was only finished a year before Isabella herself passed away. Just as unusual is the chantry on the south side of the choir that commemorates Edward Despenser, one of the original Knights of the Garter. He is shown in the unusual position here of kneeling on the roof of his tomb with a canopy over him.

The effigy of another founder knight of the Garter, Sir

Guy de Brien, Lord Welwyn and standard-bearer to Edward III at the battle of Crécy in 1346, lies on his tomb that divides the chapel of St Margaret of Scotland from the north ambulatory. He married Elizabeth Montacute after her first husband had died and the canopy of his tomb mirrors theirs, which lies directly opposite on the other side of the ambulatory.

Further round, you come across the rather gruesome cenotaph of Abbot Wakeman which stands at the entrance to the chapel of St Dunstan. On this the abbot's decaying body is shown complete with a worm, a snake, a frog, a mouse and spider or snail, crawling over it. As things turned out, Wakeman had no need of this, for he was made the first Bishop of Gloucester by Henry VIII and lies buried elsewhere.

In the Clarence vault, below the floor opposite Abbot Wakeman's cenotaph, lie the bones of George, Duke of Clarence and his wife Isabelle. He was Clarence who was reputedly drowned in a butt of malmsey.

In the southern ambulatory the sacristy is entered by a fascinating door lined with iron plates on its inner side. These are said to have been made from armour gathered from those who fell in the battle of 1471.

To add to its historical credentials the abbey possesses the oldest organ in use in the country. This is the Milton organ, built originally for Magdalen College, Oxford. However, Oliver Cromwell had it removed to Hampton Court, where it seems highly likely that John Milton would have played it during his time as Latin Secretary. For good measure, Tewkesbury Abbey has two other organs besides.

St Mary, Tickhill, South Yorkshire

In its heyday the castle at Tickhill was one of the most important fortresses in the north of England, guarding the southern approaches to Yorkshire. The castle has gone now, demolished by Cromwell's troops, but St Mary's church still stands proudly over the surrounding country-side to remind the visitor of the status that medieval Tickhill once enjoyed.

In the last quarter of the 14th century the castle was held by John of Gaunt and it seems probable that he was connected with the extensive rebuilding of the original church. This included the enlarging of the aisles and the provision of bigger windows. The great west window was built between the tower buttresses. At the other end of the nave a window was created over the chancel arch, and the window at the east of the chancel was enlarged as well. In the nave the pillars and arcades were redesigned and a lofty *clerestory* added. On the exterior, porches were built over the north and south doors, an upper storey was added to the tower as a belfry stage and the new work was finished with its distinctive parapet and pinnacles. The result of all this work was to create one of the finest medieval churches in Yorkshire.

Until the Reformation St Mary's would have been richly decorated, with a *rood screen*, coloured glass and screens of wood or fabric that partitioned off the four *chantry* chapels. Come the reigns of Edward VI and Elizabeth I

249

most of these decorative features were removed. The rood screen was almost certainly demolished and the chantries dissolved. The glass at Tickhill suffered grievously as well; the best of what remains from damage and neglect can be seen in the windows of the south aisle.

Among its tombs and memorials St Mary's includes one of the earliest examples in England of a tomb in the style of the Italian renaissance. Though considerably damaged, this commemorates Sir Thomas Fitzwilliam and his wife Lucy Neville, and dates from the first quarter of the 16th century. This tomb is similar to that of Sir Anthony Browne at Battle (page 25). After Sir Thomas Fitzwilliam's death in 1497, Lucy Neville married Sir Anthony Browne and it was their son who built the Battle tomb in the 1540s. Both tombs are worked from alabaster which, in the case of Tickhill at any rate, probably came from Chellaston in Derbyshire.

Of the single features that distinguish St Mary's the tower is paramount. This rises to a height of 124 feet and is decorated, as Alec Clifton-Taylor describes, 'With niched and canopied sculpture in the middle stage. The exuberant crown has, in addition to eight crocketed pinnacles, a pretty fringe-like parapet that has no parallel in the South: the effect is produced by erecting a little crocketed arch over each embrasure.' Restored a decade ago, the tower retains its graceful proportions and beckons worshippers and visitors to admire and experience the church's light and spacious interior.

All Saints, Trull, Somerset

All Saints, Trull, can be described as a treasure chest of medieval church art. The church itself is largely Perpendicular in style, with the base of the tower, the oldest part, dating from the middle of the 13th century.

Its principal 'treasures' come from the late Middle Ages, however. There is a *rood screen* of the fan-vaulted type that originated in Devon. Two *parclose screens* erected in memory of Thomas Keene, vicar from 1500 to 1525, are works of particularly beautiful carving.

Perhaps the church's most celebrated feature is its mid-16th-century pulpit which carries the figures of the four so-called Doctors (or learned men) of the western church and St John the Evangelist. The latter is shown holding a cup with a serpent. The four 'Doctors' are Pope Gregory (540–604), who sent St Augustine's mission to England and established Christianity in the country, an earlier St Augustine (of Hippo, 354–430), the greatest theologian of the early church, St Jerome (342–420), who translated the Bible into Latin and St Ambrose (339–397), who left the church his hymns and the ritual that bears his name.

Further fine carving is found in the bench ends made early in the 16th century by Simon Warman, who signed the work. Five of the figures seem to represent a church procession, except that they are scattered between the north and south aisles. Near the pulpit is a bench end designed with the implements of Christ's Passion.

251

Trull is also fortunate in retaining a good deal of its medieval glass, particularly in the so-called Dragon Window in the south wall of the sanctuary, which shows in late 15th-century glass St Margaret, St Michael and St George all in the act of killing dragons. Other displays of glass from the same period are dotted about the church, easily distinguished from that added during restoration work.

The golden ball surmounting St Lawrence, West Wycombe, stands out distinctively in the Buckinghamshire countryside.

St Mary the Virgin, Painswick (above), is famous for its yew trees and table-top tombs while the early twelfth-century lead font is an important feature in St Peter and St Paul, Dorchester-on-Thames (below right). Rycote Chapel, Rycote (below left), is set in rural Oxfordshire at its best.

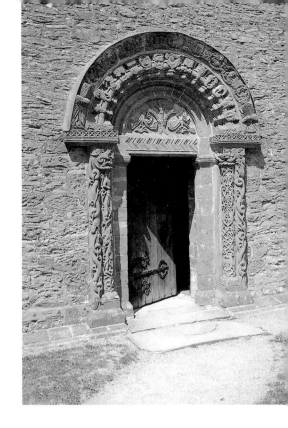

The exuberantly carved south doorway to St Mary and St David, is unique in style to the Norman sandstone church at Kilpeck. Below right is the handsome oak screen at Holy Trinity and St Mary, Abbey Dore.

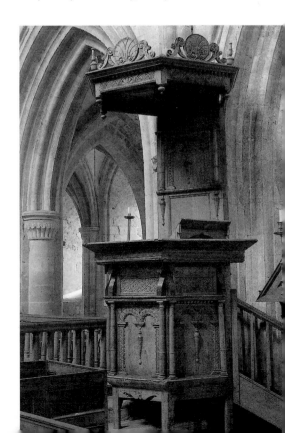

The eighteenth-century church of St Michael, Great Witley, was built as part of the Foley family's estate.

St Peter, Walpole St Peter, Norfolk

5 MILES NORTH-EAST OF WISBECH, OFF A47

Many country churches – many of them covered in this book – may possess individual features that excel any single one at Walpole St Peter but, taking the church as a whole, few can match the sense of perfect harmony and balance, of delicacy and detail, that has made Walpole St Peter not simply one of the most celebrated churches in a county famed for fine churches, but one of the most admired in the whole country.

In one respect the church owes its immensely satisfying uniformity of design to an accident, or act of God if you prefer, which befell it in 1337 when a catastrophic sea-flood destroyed all but the lower part of the tower of the earlier church. This one remnant was incorporated into the new building, which explains its slightly plainer and more modest appearance alongside the wonderful Perpendicular church that rose on the site of the old one. At the same time, a shift in local agriculture from arable farming to sheep rearing generated the resources capable of paying for a church of such noble proportions; from end to end St Peter's is over 160 feet long.

The present nave, built on the foundations of the earlier church in about 1360, served as both nave and chancel until the fine chancel was added a little over half a century later. This dual use explains why the three eastern bays of the nave (the former chancel) are narrower than the four western ones.

The nave windows are clear, glazed with glass over two hundred years old. The arches still show the beauty of the Early English pointed arch and the light grey stone blends gently with the colour wash of the walls. Unusually there is a western screen which, like the nave pews, dates from around 1630. The pulpit and intricately carved cover come from the turn of the 17th century. There is also a handsome two-tiered Dutch chandelier which was apparently bought for £33 in 1701!

The doors at the west end of the nave are the original 15th-century ones. There is a large table there, too, which may have carried refreshments for the congregation who had walked some distance to church, and a shelter once used by the priest conducting funeral services.

Moving towards the long aisleless chancel, the chancel screen survives only in its painted panels which were probably erected in the middle of the 15th century; the rest of the screen was dismantled in 1730. On the north side is the door by which access was gained to the singers' loft over the screen, while on the south side a door set slightly higher at one time gave access to the *rood beam*.

At the east end of the chancel the altar is raised ten steps above the nave to allow a vaulted passage to pass underneath, maintaining an ancient right of way that would otherwise have been blocked when the chancel was built. Functional as these steps may originally have been intended to be, they achieve a wonderful aesthetic effect, providing a fine architectural point of climax. The stone canopies over the stalls, with their delightful carvings of animals' heads and tiny bosses, are another rare feature to be found in a parish church.

The bosses in the south porch have earned much praise as well for the quality of their carving and, taken as a whole, the porch displays the best of the Perpendicular style. There are some well-carved gargoyles and corbel heads, with some on the chancel having carved bodies too, which again makes St Peter's unusual. In the 'Bolt Hole', the local name for the passage under the high altar, the carving of a sheep's head stands as a proud reminder of the source of the funds that created this superb church, and to remind us of the masons whose craftsmanship continues to draw praise and admiration. The interior of the church has approaching thirty different mason's marks on view, including that of the master mason named Hammond, whose mark can be seen on the sill of the north-west window of the north aisle.

St Werburgh, Warburton, Greater Manchester

The old church of St Werburgh is of great interest serving, as one commentator put is, as 'a monument to the inhabitants for a thousand years'.

There was probably a Saxon church on the site, but no documentary or archaeological evidence exists to confirm this. The building that stands now is timber-framed, with some walls replaced with stone in 1645 and others with brick in 1711, the date of building of the brick tower, oddly positioned in the east.

When it was first built the church originally covered the area of the present nave. The timbers of the walls and rafters are said to be pegged with deer horn and the nave pillars, now free of the plaster that encased them at one time, are of oak hardened with age.

Towards the end of the 16th century a lean-to aisle was built of sandstone on the north side of the then chancel. A short time later the other side of the chancel was extended and the little chancel and vestry were added, built with sandstone with brick in the upper courses (similar to the method later used to build the tower).

Early in the 18th century a gallery was added, as the square holes in the pillars that housed the beam supporting it show. In the mid-19th century tiles were laid on the floor of the chancel. Its ceiling was painted to represent the sky with the sun, moon and stars, and the walls were decorated with paint and stencils. At the same time the gallery was taken down and the pillars encased in plaster.

Ten years after these embellishments, the nave ceiling was stripped to expose the old beams and rafters. The oak pillars retained their plaster but were incongruously painted brown to match the natural timber above them. It was some time after that before the plaster casts were finally removed to restore the oak pillars to their original condition.

The octagonal font, cut from a single piece of sandstone, dates from the beginning of the 17th century. The hexagonal pulpit is contemporary with it and shows conventional Elizabethan designs on its carved panels. At the time of the first restoration in 1645 an early Tudor oak dining-table was installed in the church to act as a Communion table.

The graveyard has several gravestones with curious inscriptions and standing not far from a large yew tree is an 18th-century sundial, incongruously placed in its shade.

St Mary, West Walton, Norfolk

3 MILES NORTH OF WISBECH, OFF A47

St Mary's, West Walton, is one of the best Early English churches in the country and together with the church of Walpole St Peter (which is only just along the road) and other fine churches in the area, it marks a highlight in medieval church architecture.

The approach to St Mary's is made particularly striking by the magnificent detached tower which stands sixty feet away from the church. With four open arches at the base, this serves as a superb lychgate as you enter the churchyard. Slightly later than the main building, it is a fitting introduction to the glorious interior lying inside the lovely south porch.

The porch is a delightful piece of work in itself, with a perfect pointed arch flanked by two octagonal columns and decorated with two rows of dog-tooth ornaments. The inner door has four columns with carved capitals, and above the whole porch there once rose a schoolroom which no doubt disappeared when the south aisle was enlarged.

The proportions of the west end have been adversely affected by the necessity to build two huge buttresses to shore up the western bays of the nave. Even so, the beautiful double doors still remain a handsome feature reminiscent of the western doors of Salisbury Cathedral in miniature.

In the main body of the church the visitor finds some of the very best Early English work in the country. The beautiful arcading in the nave is supported on Purbeck marble piers, around which stand detached clusters of banded shafts surmounted by capitals carved with the leafy natural foliage that developed from the Early English *stiff-leaf* style.

Above the arcading runs the *clerestory*, dating from almost the same time but plainly the work of different hands. The south wall retains traces of its original painting, too, along with other elements added in the 18th century.

The chancel was modified early in the 19th century, the east wall and window having been rebuilt and the whole chancel shortened by as much as ten feet. This work destroyed the lovely double *piscina* referred to by earlier admirers of the church. The unusual eight *sedilia* remain in place however, four on the north wall, four on the south, providing seating for eight of the monks based at West Walton, while the three remaining brethren celebrated mass at the high altar.

The natural perils faced by marshland churches like this at West Walton are highlighted by the 17th-century 'flood board' that hangs in the church and records three disastrous inundations in November 1613, March 1614 and September 1671.

St Lawrence, West Wycombe, Buckinghamshire

5 MILES NORTH OF M40 EXIT 4

Six hundred feet above sea level on the hill opposite West Wycombe Park, St Lawrence's church stands out distinctively thanks to the great golden ball that surmounts its tower.

Though almost exclusively 18th century in its present manifestation, this, like so many other churches, stands on a site that has been inhabited since ancient times, the hilltop location providing a perfect vantage-point over the Wycombe valley and the important thoroughfare through the Chiltern hills that ran along it. The remains of Iron Age fortifications are still in evidence, surrounding a site of two and a half acres with a single ditch within which lie the church, the mausoleum and the churchyard.

It seems likely that a pagan temple once stood on the site, later replaced by a Saxon church when Christianity finally took hold in the area. Although nothing is known about the church until the 13th century, it's fair to surmise that it followed a familiar pattern of development through the Norman period. The present chancel belongs to the 13th century and it is here that history takes over from speculation.

In the 14th century the tower was added, probably a short, somewhat squat, structure typical of the period. The lower part remains, topped by Sir Francis

Dashwood's extravagant embellishments, and this flint and *clunch* section together with the chancel walls form the oldest parts of the present church.

By the middle of the 18th century the church was in serious need of restoration. In 1752 Sir Francis Dashwood (one of this country's more colourful Chancellors of the Exchequer, who turned the caves under his land into the notorious demesne of the Hellfire Club, and adorned West Wycombe with a number of other eccentricities) turned his attention to the church of St Lawrence and, in spite of the questionable addition of the golden ball on the tower (of which more presently), created one of the most charming and beautifully executed interiors of any contemporary church in the country.

The work of restoration was carried out painstakingly over a period of ten years and when the church was finally opened to public scrutiny one observer described it as 'the most beautiful country church in England'.

The nave was designed along the lines of the Temple of the Sun at Palmyra, near Damascus, which had been built some 1,300 years earlier. The floor and that of the chancel are of marble, widely admired for its colouring and patterns. The walls are lined with sixteen columns of imitation porphyry. These are topped by exquisitely carved Corinthian capitals that lead the eye up to the frieze, again beautifully worked in high relief. Delicate swags of flowers and foliage lie between the columns just below their capitals and above these are charming motifs of doves and olive branches and cherubs playing lyres.

Overlying all of this is the wonderful painted ceiling, which surely justifies its reputation as one of the very best in the country. From below the details of the panels and the sun-ray pattern in the centre appear to be picked out in relief although the ceiling is in fact completely flat.

The nave has three carved mahogany stalls, set imposingly like thrones on their podiums. The font is very unusual, consisting of a mahogany pillar up which climbs a serpent. On the top of this sits a silver bowl surrounded by four doves symbolically drinking the waters of life.

The royal coat of arms under which you pass into the chancel is that of George III. Inside the wrought-iron gateway, the chancel was also redesigned at the same time as the nave. In the centre of the ceiling is a painting showing the Last Supper; it is by Giovanni Borgnis, whose father had also worked on the interior of the church as well as the manor house. Other cosmopolitan features in the chancel include the altar frontal in its gilded frame, which is thought be Spanish dating from the end of the 15th century (at about the time when Columbus first sailed to America). The east window contains Flemish painted medallions of Bible scenes.

The golden ball on top of the tower is the principal attraction for most of the visitors to St Lawrence's. Built of wood and covered with gilded material it is said to have accommodated eight people playing cards, although Sir Francis Dashwood and his guests are also known to have met in a room in the tower, which would certainly have offered them greater comfort. Whatever its true purpose, the golden ball must have offered an unmatchable view across the surrounding countryside.

St Mary, Whalley, Lancashire

The Celtic crosses in Whalley churchyard point to the village as being a Christian centre before the Norman Conquest, though the attribution of the crosses to St Augustine, made by the medieval monks of Whalley Abbey, seems hard to substantiate. An association with a Scottish mission from the island of Iona at some time in the 10th century looks more likely.

St Mary's is a large church mainly built in the Early English style with a Perpendicular tower, *clerestory* and aisle windows.

The chancel, built in the first twenty years of the 13th century, is the oldest part of the church. The pillars of the chancel arch slope outwards, with something of a Middle Eastern air about them, though their alignment (or lack of it) was probably due to an error of judgement on the part of the masons. The *reredos*, altar cross and communion rails are 20th century but the stained-glass heraldic shields of the east window date from 1816 and show the arms of notable families in the neighbourhood. The pre-Reformation glass almost certainly showed a range of sacred subjects together with memorials of those buried in the church, but these must have been destroyed and, given the abundance of poor Victorian glass in so many other churches, perhaps the heraldic devices at Whalley are a suitable compromise linking, as they do, the history of the church with its present-day congregation.

The principal attraction for many visitors to Whalley church are the magnificent canopied choir-stalls carved for the abbey of Whalley in about 1430 and brought to St Mary's a little over a century later when the abbey was dissolved. With only a few minor exceptions, the stalls represent the choir seating of the Cistercian monks as it was originally created by a local carver named Eatough, whose family name can still be found in the parish.

The beautifully worked *misericords* show a wide range of subjects, from roses and pigs beneath an oak tree to the sacred subjects of a pelican feeding her young with her own blood and an angel carrying more flowers. As with all misericords, each shows a distinctive view of the medieval imagination, both lay and clerical, which the carver was able to exercise rather more freely than in the more formal displays of his skill around the church.

The chancel screen is a couple of hundred years younger than the choir-stalls and originally had a *rood loft* above that was wide enough to support an altar and which would have been reached by a spiral staircase.

The nave was built later in the 13th century, during a period of transition between the Early English style and the Decorated style that succeeded it. Pointed Early English arches form the four bays on each side of the nave leading to the north and south aisles, though the pillars on the north side are cylindrical while those on the south are octagonal, reflecting the interesting change in style that was taking place as church architecture finally moved away from the Romanesque influence of the Norman period that had governed it for well over two centuries.

The nave roof is a substantial, elegant structure erected in the late 15th century and decorated with fine bosses.

On the south side of the nave is a large pew separated from the rest of the church by a beautiful carved screen from the 16th century and known, not unreasonably, as 'the cage', an ancient term for pews like this that some-times served as chapels.

In the front of the pulpit is another lovely piece of wood-carving forming the Starkie pew, which dates from the early 18th century.

The font was carved from the same yellow gritstone used to form the pillars of the nave and, in spite of being a couple of centuries younger, has acquired the same warm patina. Its oak cover is two hundred years younger still and carries the marks of the lock which once fastened it to protect the baptismal water inside, because this was believed to have healing powers and was frequently pinched to be offered to the sick of the parish.

The magnificent organ at the west end of the nave was originally built for Lancaster Priory in 1727, but found its way to Whalley in 1813.

Both north and south aisles have chapels that were originally *chantries*, founded when the hermitage that used to stand in the churchyard was dissolved in the middle of the 15th century, apparently because the then inmate fell short of her duties in some way. The hermit-age had been founded in 1361 to provide shelter, servants, a priest to say mass daily, and a good supply of food to a female recluse. When the last recluse departed some eighty years later, the endowments passed to Whalley Abbey on the understanding that priests came daily to say mass in the two chantries 'for the souls of King Henry VI and his descendants'. This practice lasted for twenty-five years after chantries had officially been abolished and the names of some of the priests who perpetuated it, Christopher Smith, Thomas Lawe and Thomas Harwood, are recorded in the church.

St Mary's has a number of interesting tombs from all periods of its history, and a collection of chained books in a case at the west end of the north aisle.

St Mary, Whitby, North Yorkshire

16 MILES NORTH-WEST OF SCARBOROUGH, OFF A171

The old port (and more recent seaside holiday town) of Whitby lies on either side of the River Esk, backed by the brooding presence of the North York Moors away to the west. The old town lies nestled below the East Cliff topped by the ruins of the great abbey which has stood as a landmark for sailors up and down the coast for centuries. Close by stands St Mary's church which dates from around 1110 though, as the visitor soon discovers, much has happened to it since then.

The Norman church was most likely built on the site of the Saxon church of St Peter constructed in 657 to serve the monastery founded by Oswy, King of Northumbria, whose first abbess was St Hilde, or Hilda to give her her modern name. It was here that the Synod of Whitby was convened to decide whether the Roman or Celtic Church should prevail in determining the date of Easter; as history shows, the Roman Church won the day.

St Hilda's monastery was also the home of Caedmon, the Anglo-Saxon herdsman who became the earliest known English poet when he received a vision that empowered him with the gift of composing verse. Several poems are attributed to him, but the hymn on the Creation recorded by Bede is regarded as the most authentic. Near the edge of the churchyard overlooking the old town stands the cross erected in Caedmon's honour and unveiled in 1898 by the Poet Laureate, Alfred Austin.

This is based on the design of the preaching cross at Ruthwell on the Solway Firth, which appears from its runic inscription to have had some link with Caedmon. The cross in Whitby shows the figures of Christ, King David, Caedmon in his stable and Abbess Hilda. She is shown standing on snakes, a reference to the local legend which credits her with saving the town from an infestation of snakes by cutting off their heads and turning them into stone. This is meant to explain the great range of ammonites found in the cliffs around Whitby; some in the museum measure almost a metre across.

The original Saxon church of St Peter was destroyed by Danish invaders in the 9th century, though evidence from the Domesday Book and other sources suggests that the site was occupied by one or more later churches during the two centuries between then and the building of the present church. Although St Mary's has received many obvious additions down the ages, it has never had aisles, unlike so many other churches enlarged to cater for growing congregations; here galleries were added when further space was needed. Since the extension of the north-west side in 1819 the seating capacity has been 1500.

The north and south transepts were added in about 1225 and 1380 respectively, transforming the church to a cruciform shape in which it remained until the 19th century.

The Norman chancel arch was virtually obscured in the early 17th century by the extraordinary gallery built by the all-powerful lords of the manor, and named the Cholmley Pew after them. Standing on legs that look like twists of barley sugar this occupies the most conspicuous place in the church, which in the Middle Ages had formerly housed a *rood screen*.

At about the same time St Mary's also acquired its equally individual roof, when the old high-pitched roof was replaced by a flat roof. This looks so strikingly like the deck of a ship that it seems almost certain that it was built by ships' carpenters. (If this is the case, it would be particularly appropriate since the word 'nave' is derived from the Latin noun *navis* meaning a ship.)

Towards the end of the 17th century the first of the general galleries was built along the south wall of the nave. Others followed over the next hundred years, along with further alterations that transformed St Mary's into something unlike any other church in the country.

The three-decker pulpit which immediately catches your eye as you enter was constructed in 1778 and originally stood on iron props, under which the congregation walked to reach the east end of the church. It was moved to its present position in 1847. The preaching box on the upper level is used for delivering the sermon; the middle deck is occupied by the priest taking the service; while the lower level accommodates the parish clerk, sitting beside his wand of office.

Whitby's historic association with the sea is well represented in various features in the church. In the porch stands the model of an ancient Greek temple installed by the Reverend W. Keane, Rector of Whitby at the time of the great storm of 9 February 1861 in which twelve of the thirteen-man crew of Whitby's lifeboat were drowned agonizingly close to shore and in full view of thousands of townspeople.

On the left of the sanctuary stands a beautifully carved chair made from the timbers of a ship called the *Royal Charter*. This is known as the Scoresby Chair, named after one of Whitby's most famous mariners, William Scoresby, whaler and polar explorer. His father, also named William Scoresby, was the inventor of the crow's-nest and William Scoresby the younger made important improvements to the magnetic compass which were adopted by the Royal Navy. After being ordained in

1826, he furthered his interest in navigation – this led to his voyage in the *Royal Charter* in 1856, when he sailed to Antarctica to measure the effect of iron-hulled ships on magnetic compasses and to recommend appropriate adjustments. The chair was made after the *Royal Charter* was wrecked three years later, and was presented to St Mary's in 1922.

The bronze statue of Whitby's other great seafarer, Captain James Cook, stands on the West Cliff of the town, opposite the church. Although Cook was not born in Whitby, he learned much of his early seamanship here and his ships *Resolution*, *Endeavour*, *Discovery* and *Adventure* were all built in the town. Attending services in St Mary's, the young Cook would have sat in the west gallery alongside his fellow apprentices.

Among its tombs and memorials the churchyard has a couple which attract particular attention. One just outside the chancel door commemorates Francis and Mary Huntrodds, who were both born on 19 September 1600, were married on their birthday and died within five hours of each other on their eightieth birthday.

On the seaward side of the church is a stone seat with eerie associations with Dracula. The novelist Bram Stoker was staying in Whitby while working on his spine-chilling novel and apparently some of the most exciting and horrific chapters were written after a nightmare brought on by eating crab for supper! The seat in the churchyard is very similar to that on which Stoker sat his heroine Lucy one night, while Dracula hovered in the background in the shape of a large dog.

St Candida and Holy Cross, Whitchurch Canonicorum, Dorset

The peaceful village of Whitchurch Canonicorum lies in the heart of Marshwood Vale, only a couple of miles from the English Channel, but screened from the sea by a range of steep hills. Its approach is by winding lanes banked by hedgerows, so evocative of a tranquil rural backwater that it comes as a surprise to learn that the parish still encompasses over fifty farms and was once one of the largest in England.

The village was probably founded during the reign of Alfred the Great. He certainly left it to his youngest son Ethelwald in his will at the end of the 9th century.

The importance attached to Whitchurch persisted for a further two centuries. William the Conqueror appointed Guntard, his personal chaplain, to the benefice when he first took control of his new kingdom and when Guntard became a monk at the abbey dedicated to St Wandrille in Normandy, the living was transferred there.

Monks from Guntard's abbey were responsible for dismantling the old Saxon church and beginning work on a new Norman building. Subsidence caused them problems, as examination of the western pier of the central rounded arch in the south arcade reveals.

In the closing years of the 12th century the benefice changed hands again, to the Bishop of Sarum this time, and it is thanks to the builders appointed by him that Whitchurch Canonicorum now possesses one of the finest examples of Early English work in the county. In their hands the north arcade, the chancel arch and chancel, the transepts and the shrine (which we'll come to in a moment) were all crafted and embellished with beautifully and deeply cut capitals, each with its own design of flowers and foliage. There are good examples, too, of Early English arches in the north arcade.

At around the beginning of the 15th century the last great building phase began in which the fine Perpendicular tower, the porch, the battlements on the south wall, the arches into the tower and transepts and the barrel roofs of the nave and north transept were all added.

These are the architectural qualities that attract the visitor to this charming country church. However, St Candida and Holy Cross possesses one feature that makes it unique among English parish churches. Beneath the north window of the north transept is the shrine of St Wite (St Candida to give her her Latin, and probably erroneous, name) which still contains her authenticated bones, making this the only parish church in the country still to possess its patroness's relics. (This was confirmed in the winter of 1899–90 when movements in the surrounding masonry opened an ancient crack in the tomb chest, permitting investigators access to the lead casket inside. This contained the bones of a woman aged about forty and bore a Latin inscription confirming that they were the relics of St Wite.)

The shrine dates from the early 13th century. It is built into the wall and formed in two parts: an upper tomb chest in Purbeck marble, which contains the relics, and a lower portion with three large oval openings. Through these pilgrims would thrust their diseased limbs, or pieces of cloth to be taken away as healing bandages for sick friends or relatives. In return they also brought offerings:

a candle, a coin, sometimes items of food like cakes or cheeses.

That the shrine survived intact after the Reformation, when almost every other was destroyed, remains a mystery. So does the true identity of the saint herself. Until the last century it was generally held that St Wite fell victim to one of the savage Danish coastal raids that terrorized southern England during the 9th century. Then opposing theories were put forward that she might have been a Breton saint, brought to these shores after the Viking conquest of Brittany in the 10th century, or that St Wite was in fact a monk named Witta, who travelled from the West Country with St Boniface of Crediton in his mission to convert the people of Germany.

Contemporary opinion seems now to be running in favour of the original concept of St Wite as a simple Anglo-Saxon hermit living and ending her days in and around this stretch of the Dorset coast.

Whatever her true identity, faith in her powers of aiding the sick survive to this day. Coins and requests for help before operations, or to succour sick friends and relatives, are still found in the base of this shrine which has been a place of pilgrimage for over nine hundred years.

St Cuthburga, Wimborne Minster, Dorset

The Romans were the first to settle at Wimborne Minster. They were followed by the Saxons who developed the site and in AD 713 St Cuthburga, sister of King Ina of the West Saxons, founded a Benedictine nunnery in the town which at one time had five hundred women training for missionary work under its roof. In the 9th and 10th centuries Danish raids were launched against the town and the surrounding area from Poole Harbour. In one of these in 871 King Ethelred (not the Unready) was killed defending his kingdom from the invaders at nearby Martin, and was buried in the minster by his younger brother and successor, King Alfred. In 1013 the Danes destroyed the nunnery itself and it was never rebuilt. Thirty years after this, Edward the Confessor established a college of secular canons which lasted until 1547.

In spite of 19th-century restoration, the minster preserves much of its original grandeur and the many features that have attracted visitors for hundreds of years.

Dominating the centre of the town, the minster is immediately distinguishable by its twin towers: one at the western end and one in the centre. The western tower was added in 1464 with the express purpose of housing a peal of five bells that has been added to over the centuries and is now double the original number.

The central tower stands on four huge Norman arches built at about 1120 which now form the oldest part of the church. The three upper storeys were constructed towards the end of the 12th century, and were originally topped by a spire until one day in 1600 when that was 'strangely cast down' in a 'mist'. The nave arcades are largely Norman, too, in spite of their pointed arches on which the zigzag decoration is very unusual. The small round-headed windows above the nave arches originally formed the *clerestory* of the Norman church before the roof was raised; the line of the old roof can be seen in traces on the west wall of the central tower.

In the baptistery at the other end of the church stands the late Norman font, carved from Purbeck marble and supported by eight cylindrical shafts. The baptistery also houses the fascinating 14th-century astronomical clock, designed and built before Copernicus corrected the mistaken belief that the earth lies in the centre of the universe. Accordingly the sun revolves around the outer circle of the 24-hour clock acting as an hour hand, while the moon in the inner circle shows the phase of the lunar month. On the outside of the west tower a quarter-jack, dressed as grenadier at the time of the Napoleonic wars, strikes two bells every quarter-hour. Back inside the baptistery, on the north wall, is a tombstone to one of the county's most enterprising and daring smugglers, a chap named Gulliver, who had many close shaves with the Revenue men but ended his days peacefully settled in Wimborne.

The wooden panelling in the west end of the north aisle marks the site of the old Consistory Court where wills were proved and church law administered. Further eastwards along the north aisle is St Cuthburga's window, which shows Wimborne's patron saint holding a model of the minster.

St George's chapel at the eastern end of the north side of the minster contains a number of interesting features. Originally used by a local guild of wool merchants at the end of the 15th century, it contains the fine renaissance monument to Sir Edmund Uvedale erected by his widow following his death in 1606. The Italian sculptor of the work portrayed Sir Edmund with opening eyes, suggesting his awakening at his own resurrection. Fortunately the knight is shown lying with his head propped on one elbow, for if he tried walking in his present state he might have some difficulty: due to an error in restoration poor Sir Edmund was given two left feet!

The chapel also houses a Saxon oak chest hewn from a solid trunk which is believed to be some 1,100 years old. The other two chests housed minster records, among them accounts dating back to 1475.

From St George's chapel steps lead down into the crypt, which contains the Lady chapel built in about 1340. Up the steps on the south side is the Holy Trinity chapel which contains the tomb of Anthony Ettricke, Recorder and Magistrate of Poole from 1662 until 1682, who in his old age took a disliking to the people of Wimborne and vowed that 'he would never be buried within the church or without it – neither below the ground nor above it'. However, a later change of heart coupled with some shrewd legal brainwork enabled him to be buried with his ancestors without losing face. This he achieved by obtaining permission to create a recess in the wall where his coffin could be placed. He was definitely wrong on one point nevertheless. Having been totally convinced that he would die in 1693 he had his coffin inscribed with this date. When he wasn't called to meet his Maker until ten years later the date had to be changed, as is easily spotted.

Other interesting tombs and memorials are found in the chancel where Henry VII's grandparents, John de

Beaufort, Duke of Somerset, and his Duchess lie as fine effigies on their alabaster tomb. On the north wall just beyond the sanctuary step is the 15th-century memorial brass to Alfred's brother, King Ethelred, the only memorial brass effigy of an English king in existence.

Above the choir vestry is Wimborne's famous chained library founded in 1686 and comprising books from the 14th to the 17th centuries, including several notable Bibles and even the works of Machiavelli.

St Thomas the Apostle, Winchelsea, East Sussex

7 MILES NORTH-EAST OF HASTINGS, ON A259

Although Winchelsea is more than a mile from the sea, it once flourished as a seaport and was later one of the Cinque Ports. But the sea which brought Winchelsea prosperity also wrought its destruction, for the Winchelsea of today is not the original town. That was submerged by the sea, late in the 13th century, leading Edward I to establish a new town laid out on a systematic grid pattern in 1288.

The sea also carried raiders from France during the 14th century and it was they who destroyed much of the great church that stood in the centre of King Edward's new town, with the result that all that remains today of that magnificent edifice are the choir and aisles.

Even when the French raids subsided, Winchelsea was faced by the gradual loss of its trading wealth as the harbour silted up and merchants moved away. As a consequence there was little spare money to undertake repairs on the church. The diarist John Evelyn was in the town in the middle of the 17th century and found St Thomas's in 'forlorn ruins'. One hundred and fifty years later John Wesley paid a visit to what he referred to as 'that poor skeleton of Ancient Winchelsea with its large church now in ruins'. By the middle of the 19th century it was 'almost unfit for public worship' and then in 1850 urgent repairs were started and saved the ancient fabric from further deterioration in the nick of time.

Inside the north aisle three effigies, thought to have been saved from the old church in Winchelsea before it was swallowed up by the sea for ever, poignantly recall the lost town. No one knows for certain who they represent, but they are thought to have been members of the Godfrey family. The first, opposite the font, shows a knight dressed in armour. Then comes a lady, thought perhaps to have been his wife, followed by a young man wearing a long robe who may have been their son. We will probably never know their true identity, but here they lie – survivors in stone of a bygone age and a bygone town.

Dr Douglas Strachan was responsible for a considerable amount of the stained glass in the church and the restored Lady chapel has three windows designed by him above the three effigies. These form part of the church's war memorial that was dedicated by Archbishop Lang in 1933. The altar in the Lady chapel was also restored as part of the war memorial, and on the retable behind the altar are two saints with appropriate military credentials: St Martin of Tours who, like the present Archbishop of Canterbury, was once a soldier (though in the Roman army) before becoming a bishop; and St Alban, another Roman officer and the first native of these islands who is known to have given his life in the service of Christ. St George joins them, killing a dragon, as does St Andrew of Scotland, who represents the naval arm of the memorial. In the centre is a crucifix which, like the other statues, was carved by Esmond Burton.

In the sanctuary the richly canopied *sedilia* and a *piscina* remain in the south wall, while opposite them in the north wall are two panels of 14th-century glass.

There are other *sedilia*, and another *piscina* in the south wall of the St Nicholas chapel above which is a striking window commemorating the crew of the Rye lifeboat who were lost at sea during a terrible storm on 15 November 1928; this was also the work of Douglas Strachan.

The church's sea connections take it further back in time to the early 14th century and the *chantry* established by Stephen Alard. Two tombs lie here. The more easterly is thought to be that of Gervase Alard, Admiral of the Western Fleet appointed by Edward I and as such this country's first real admiral. The other is that of Stephen Alard himself, Admiral of the Cinque Ports and the Western Fleet.

St Peter, Wootton Wawen, Warwickshire

Over the centuries St Peter's, Wootton Wawen, has been added to and has grown around the Saxon tower which stood at the centre of the cruciform church built in about 1035–40 by Wagen (or Wahen), from whom the village gained its name. An earlier church had stood on the site since 723, but nothing remains from that first building.

Following the Norman Conquest Wagen was dispossessed, a group of Norman monks arrived in his village and in due course the church was enlarged and altered. Fortunately the lower stages of the tower, supported by its four arches beneath which stands the 'Saxon Sanctuary', remained unaltered.

In the 13th century the growing congregation led to further enlargement through the building of the south aisle, a south chapel and bigger chancel. Towards the end of the 15th century the *clerestory* was added to the nave, the tower received its upper stage and the doorway was created in the north wall (to be covered by a porch in the following century).

There is a small Norman window and traces of an early Norman or Saxon doorway in the north wall. The oak *parclose screens* and pulpit were added in the 15th century, at much the same time as the windows of the clerestory. At the west end the Perpendicular window is filled with modern glass given by Herbert Hanbury Smith-Carrington of Ashby Folville, Leicestershire.

The Saxon sanctuary below the tower has been the hub of the church for nine hundred years. When first built it would have been the crossing of the church, with the main altar standing in a small chancel through the east arch.

To the south of the present chancel stands the large Lady chapel, as big as many parish churches and larger than the chancel of St Peter's. This has fragments of ancient wall paintings, a number of interesting monuments (among them the tomb of Francis Smith, which shows the figure of a man dressed in armour) and the gravestone covering the poet William Somerville, who died in 1742, inscribed with an epitaph which he composed himself.

Through the 15th-century wooden screen lies the chancel, with a lovely window in the east wall containing glass from the 14th and 15th centuries. Traces of the south window, which was closed up when the Lady chapel was built, can be seen along with part of the *sedilia*. Today wrought-iron gates in the chancel arch and a curtain drawn across them blank off the chancel and its fine window during the chilly months of winter, leaving the Saxon sanctuary, with its comparatively recent altar, to act as the focal point of the church.

St Mary The Virgin, Yatton, Avon

For miles around St Mary's, Yatton, stands out against the skyline thanks to its distinctive truncated spire and its noble high nave that has earned it the nickname of 'The Cathedral of the Moors'.

A Norman church stood on the site and a Saxon one before that, but when major rebuilding work began in the 1320s all traces of these earlier buildings disappeared except for the cruciform shape of the Norman church which was retained by the medieval builders, who placed their new tower at the intersection. Today the four huge arches of the crossing are the oldest parts of the church, their mouldings having been added in the 15th century.

As it was originally designed in the 14th century, the nave of St Mary's would probably have been of similar proportions to the present chancel. But in the second half of the 15th century the parishioners replaced this by the lofty and considerably lengthened nave that lends a certain majesty to the church today. Early churchwardens' accounts show the pride taken in the new structure by the people of the parish, and this would have been further enhanced by the carved and gilded *rood screen* that ran right across the church and was decorated by sixty-nine painted statues and a large figure of Christ on the cross. Like so many others in England, this was completely destroyed in the middle of the 16th century.

One piece of decoration that can still be found is the face of the Green Man carved on the capital topping the most easterly pillar on the north side of the nave. Among the formal carved foliage, this throwback to pagan beliefs peers out as a reminder of primitive rites and faiths.

There are more conventional examples of the medieval craftsman's skill to be seen in the north transept, formerly known as the De Wyck chapel, after one of the two great families of the neighbourhood. In the wall are a couple of recessed wall tombs surmounted by Tudor canopies. There are also the much damaged, but still impressive, effigies of Sir Richard Newton (a member of the other prominent Yatton family) and his wife, lying on a table-tomb in the centre.

The Newton chapel itself lies further east, built in the closing years of the 15th century by Sir Richard's daughter-in-law, Lady Isabel Cheddar. She was also the generous benefactress who made possible the building of Yatton's celebrated south porch at about the same time. Pevsner describes this as the most highly decorated in Somerset, and its beautiful panels and vaulting make it one of the church's chief attractions.

The church also possesses a lovely piece of 15th-century embroidery made from two velvet vestments which covered the parish coffin when that was used at funerals. This is now mounted behind glass and is a rare example of pre-Reformation work of this quality.

Glossary

Ambulatory – A place for walking; a continuation of the aisled spaces on either side of the nave around the apse or chancel to form a continuous processional way.

Apse – Rounded (semicircular or polygonal) end to a chancel or chapel.

Aumbry – Small recess or cupboard to hold sacred vessels for mass or communion.

Broach (spire) – Half-pyramid of stone or wood set above each angle of a square, unparapeted tower to effect the transition to a tapering octagonal spire.

Cartouche – Tablet with a device or inscription framed by carved scrolls.

Cellarium – Store-room or cellar.

Celure – Canopy or specially adorned section of a roof over an altar or rood.

Chantry (chapel) – Chapel endowed by a founder for the chanting of masses for his soul, or by a guild for its members.

Clerestory – A 'clear' storey – the upper part of the wall of a church, usually in the nave, with a row of windows above the aisle roofs.

Clunch – Hard chalk used for intricate carving inside a church, liable to weather badly externally.

Corbel – Stone bracket projecting from a wall.

Corbel-table – Row of corbels supporting a parapet or cornice.

Cornice – Uppermost, most prominent wall moulding.

Crocket – Leaf-shaped projection used as decoration.

Doom – Depiction of the Last Judgement, usually painted over a chancel arch.

Groined roof (or vault) – Roof or vault formed from the intersection of two semicircular vaults at right angles. The groins are the lines along the edges of the intersections.

Hatchment – Tablet with armorial bearings.

Hollis – Gallery (on a tower).

Hood-mould (also Dripstone or Label) – Projecting moulding above an arch or window to throw off water.

Label-stop – Carved ornamental head or other shape at the end of a hood-mould.

Lancet – Slender pointed window.

Lantern (tower) – Tower in which the crossing space extends upwards to be lit by windows above the level of the surrounding roofs.

Lierne – Short decorative subsidiary rib in the style of vaulting named after it.

Mass dial – Simple sundial on the south side of a church, with lines to mark the times of services.

Misericord – Bracket on the underside of hinged seat in choir-stalls, often enriched with lively carvings.

Narthex – Enclosed vestibule at the principal entrance of a church.

Palimpsest – Memorial brass used a second time.

Parclose (screen) – Screen separating a chapel or aisle from the rest of the church.

Pilaster – Rectangular column attached to and projecting from a wall.

Piscina – Shallow basin with drain near an altar, used for washing the mass or communion vessels.

Poppy-head – Leaflike or floral ornament used to decorate the tops of bench ends or choir-stalls.

Porticus – Side chamber.

Presbytery – Eastern part of the church beyond the choir.

Pulpitum – Stone screen shutting off the choir from the nave in a major church.

Quatrefoil – Four-lobed ornamental infilling for a circle or arch-head.

Quoin – Dressed stone at the angle of a building.

Reredos – Wall or screen behind the altar, usually decorated.

Rood – Rood is the Old English word for cross or crucifix.

Rood loft, rood screen – Medieval churches had a large cross, or rood, supported by a beam (the 'rood beam') spanning the nave at the entrance to the chancel. Later a rood screen was added, rising from the floor to this beam; and the rood loft, above the screen, was also added. Upon this loft, or gallery, was displayed the rood, usually with a statue (one of the Virgin Mary, one of St John) on either side. The rood loft was used by musicians and singers on special occasions, and it was reached by rood stairs, either built into the stone wall of the chancel or housed in a free-standing turret.

From the 14th century until the mid-16th century rood screens and lofts were prominent features of churches, and were often elaborately carved, painted and decorated. When Henry VIII established the Church of England in the 1530s, it was decreed that the rood and everything above the rood beam had to be removed, though the screens were allowed to remain. Further destruction of church ornamentation during the period of the Civil War and the Commonwealth (1640–60) led to further losses; later church architects preferred an unbroken view into the chancel from the nave.

Sedilia – Recessed stone seats in the chancel for the priest and his assistants.

Slype – Covered passage-way from a transept or cloister of a cathedral or monastic church to the chapter house or deanery.

Spandrel – Triangular wall surface in the angle between two arches.

Springer – Support from which an arch springs.

Stiff-leaf – Early English type of foliage with stiff stems and lobed leaves.

Tabernacle – Elaborately ornamented niche or free-standing canopy.

Triforium – Arcaded wall passage or area of blank arcading above the main arcade of a church and below the clerestory.

Tympanum – Space in the head of a doorway arch.

Triptych – Picture or carving (or set of three) side by side with hinged lateral panels that fold over the central one, often used as an altarpiece.

County index